Working with children who have experienced neglect

Victoria Sharley and Alyson Rees

Published by
CoramBAAF Adoption and Fostering Academy
41 Brunswick Square
London WC1N 1AZ
www.corambaaf.org.uk

Coram Academy Limited, registered as a company limited by guarantee
in England and Wales number 9697712, part of the Coram group, charity
number 312278

British Library Cataloguing in Publication Data
A catalogue record for this book is available from the British Library

ISBN 978 1 913384 21 0

Project management by Jo Francis, Publications, CoramBAAF
Designed and typeset by Helen Joubert Design
Printed in Great Britain by The Lavenham Press

For the latest news on CoramBAAF titles and special offers, sign up to
our free publications bulletin at https://corambaaf.org.uk/subscribe.

Contents

Note about the authors

Dr Victoria Sharley

Victoria Sharley is a Senior Lecturer in Social Work with Children and Families in the School for Policy Studies at the University of Bristol. Victoria has a PhD from Cardiff University in identifying and responding to child neglect in the context of interprofessional practice with schools and is a registered social worker with a background in child and family social work, having worked in child protection, youth justice, and domestic violence and abuse services. Victoria is the Programme Director for the MSc in Social Work at the University of Bristol and an active member of the Children and Families' Research Centre. Her research interests are child neglect, schools, interprofessional practice, child care and protection in Africa.

Professor Alyson Rees

Alyson Rees is a Professor of Social Work in the School of Social Sciences at Cardiff University, and Assistant Director of CASCADE, child and family research centre. Alyson is also responsible for ExChange, a research dissemination programme (www.ExChangewales.org). She has been a practitioner for 16 years, working in criminal justice and domestic abuse. Her research interests are in children looked after, foster care, adoption, mothers in prison, and practice reviews. Alyson is a registered social worker.

Note

Please note, Chapter 2 of this book was written by Dr Julie Doughty, Senior Lecturer in Law at Cardiff University School of Law and Politics.

Acknowledgements

We would like to thank all of the busy practitioners who kindly gave of their time to provide us with case examples and talk to us about their work:

- Juanita Scallan – independent social worker, Devon

- Joel Price – social worker, Cardiff

- Olivia Clark – social worker, Devon

- Annie Fligelstone – student social worker, Bridgend

- Lindsey Warren – foster carer, Cardiff

- Dave Walker – psychotherapist, Vale of Glamorgan

- CarolAnn Stirling – social worker, Cornwall

Introduction

Neglect is the most common reason for a child to be placed on a child protection plan in the UK. In 2020, 26,010 children were registered under the category of neglect in England and a further 995 in Wales (NSPCC, 2021a). These figures account for 50 per cent of all child protection plans in England and 43 per cent of all child protection registrations in Wales. It is thought that around 1 in 10 children in the UK have been neglected (NSPCC, 2021a). In 2019, neglect was the most common form of harm for adolescents who were on the child protection register or subject to a child protection plan in England and Northern Ireland (and the second most common in Wales and Scotland) (NSPCC, 2020). There is also a clear intersection between neglect and emotional abuse; Gardner notes that: 'there is overlap between many forms of child maltreatment and this is especially true of neglect' (2008, p.15).

Responding effectively to child neglect and supporting children who are living with or have experienced neglect – whether in the care of their parents or family members, or in foster, adoptive or residential care – is widely acknowledged as a complex and challenging task for social workers and other practitioners. It often takes time, perseverance and the gathering of substantial information and evidence. During 2014–2017, neglect was present in nearly three-quarters of all serious case reviews into the death or serious harm of children (Brandon *et al*, 2020). Lessons from these reviews consistently offer the same messages and learning for practice, emphasising the biggest challenges for responding successfully to neglect to be productive and effective interprofessional communication, and information sharing across services (Child Safeguarding Practice Review Panel (CSPRP), 2020).

So why is the most prevalent form of child maltreatment so difficult to respond to in practice? What are the common challenges experienced by practitioners in providing the appropriate level of support to children living with neglect? How do we achieve effective practice in a timely and helpful manner that meets a child's needs and ensures they are sufficiently protected from harm? This book explores nine key themes that aim to unpick the complexity of working with child neglect in the form of an accessible good practice guide. The practice guide offers a summary of key messages for frontline practitioners in a clear and easy to digest format. It is intended to be used as a "go to" desk resource for busy practitioners and students working within a wide range of services that are responsible for safeguarding and protecting children and young people who are living with, or have experienced, neglect, and those who are in the process of receiving support for, or recovering from its impact.

1

STRUCTURE OF THE GUIDE

The guide begins with the early identification of neglect when children are living with their birth parents or family members, and focuses on understanding neglect as a concept, assessment, intervention, and the importance of multi-agency practice and working across services. It then moves to offering messages and guidance for how to effectively work with children who are receiving support to recover from the trauma of experiencing neglect, and who are cared for by friends, family members, foster carers, in residential care, or who have been adopted.

The guide is designed to be an applied text for a range of professionals and students in practice settings. With this in mind, it offers "real-life" case studies at the end of each chapter, which have been produced by practitioners, managers, carers, and social work students who are experienced in working with child neglect in their roles. Each chapter also includes key messages or insights that set out examples of what has worked well in practice, together with ideas and activities for use in reflective supervision. Whilst this is not an academic text, for readers who wish to access more in-depth literature, research and applied tools on the topics covered, each chapter signposts readers to additional resources and further reading that relate to the topics discussed.

NOTE ON TERMINOLOGY

There are two different types of social worker working in fostering – those who support the child (the children's social worker), and those who support the foster carer (the fostering social worker, also known as the supervising social worker).

Chapter 1
Understanding child neglect

INTRODUCTION

In its broadest sense, child neglect can be understood as a child's basic needs not being sufficiently met. However, aside from this broad definition, neglect can also be defined more narrowly in terms of legal, policy and organisational contexts (Daniel *et al*, 2014). Whilst literature on child neglect offers some simple typologies of neglect – which include categories of medical, nutritional, emotional, educational and physical neglect, and lack of supervision and guidance (Horwath, 2007; Farmer and Lutman, 2012) – effectively describing neglect is quite problematic due to its complexity (Daniel *et al*, 2011). This chapter reflects on some of the challenges of defining neglect in practice. It considers its conceptual complexity, the changing nature of neglect over time, space and culture, and why as a form of maltreatment it is often more difficult to classify and evidence compared to other types of abuse. This can mean it is often difficult to ensure that a child receives the appropriate help they need, and that the help is provided in a timely manner.

The chapter explores the impact of individual, professional, organisational, and cultural biases in our perceptions of child neglect. It acknowledges some of the conceptual differences between children and young people's understandings about what they believe constitutes neglectful parenting and how these can vary from views held by adults. Differences in conceptual and definitional understanding of child neglect can have fundamental significance for being able to notice neglect and provide the necessary support a child needs. This is particularly the case when working with a range of practitioners from different professional remits, and understandings differ widely.

WHAT IS CHILD NEGLECT?

Defining neglect

Child neglect in its simplest form can be understood as an omission of appropriate care (Stowman and Donohue, 2005; Holland *et al*, 2013), most usually by a child's parent(s) or carer(s) who is/are not meeting the child's basic needs, either emotionally or physically. It is typically characterised by the relationship between the child and parent or carer (Glaser, 2000) in the context of the child's basic needs. Other types of abuse, such as physical or sexual abuse, can be considered acts of commission where it is possible to describe the presence of the act (e.g. a child being hit or chastised at a specific moment in time). Conversely, capturing the absence or omission of care is a more challenging task for practitioners. Acts of omission could include a failure to meet the physical needs of a child such as provision of food, clothing, shelter and warmth, or failure to meet their emotional or developmental needs by neglecting to provide cognitive stimulation, adequate health care, and failing to protect a child from harm (Horwath, 2007). It could also include the failure to protect a child from harm or danger (whether living with a parent/carer or in foster or residential care) (Beesley, 2011) or radicalisation (NSPCC, 2022a).

Having the ability to identify the presence of an adequate level of care, condition, or caring behaviour (English *et al*, 2005) over a period of time raises questions about what is deemed to be acceptable, and therefore requires an understanding of what may constitute an unacceptable level of parenting or care for children in society (Horwath, 2007; 2013).

(In)adequate care – what is "good enough"?

Consequently, defining what neglectful care is requires a social judgement about what is considered a normative standard of care for a child – at a given point in society (Rees *et al*, 2011). Because neglect is not a static phenomenon, but a social construct that moves and shifts across time through the influence of cultural and ideological values (Scourfield, 2000), what may be perceived to be neglectful or in fact "good enough" care continues to change, over space and place. Perceptions and understandings of neglect can shift, either lessening or emphasising certain characteristics dependent on norms within a given culture, community, or context (Horwath, 2013). This shift can be clearly seen in recent years with children placed on child protection plans for nutritional neglect – traditionally due to malnourishment and hunger – now increasingly linked to the problem of childhood obesity, where parents and carers are positioned as accountable in children's poor diet choices, which influence the quality and quantity of the food their child consumes (Department of Health (DH), 2005). These shifts and changes hold particular relevance for responding to neglect with colleagues from different professional contexts, or working to support a child living with neglect within a multi-agency setting. Consider the challenges of a teaching assistant in a school, making a referral to a social worker in children's services, a decision that draws on their own personal experiences of how they were parented as a child.

In addition to personal and social norms, there is also a lack of agreement around statutory thresholds for intervention when a child is living with neglect. This lack of clarity not only exists between different professional disciplines such as education and social care (Sharley, 2019), but can also differ between local authorities, or nation states within the UK. Difference in thresholds for the provision of support services or legal intervention (Dickens, 2007) often vary widely across (and at times within!) teams in the same organisation (Beesley, 2011), and can be connected to the availability of resources and budgets in the area.

These differing perceptions of what is considered neglect are a manifestation of our identities, both professional and personal, and introduce a considerable challenge for practice. It is therefore not possible to agree a single definition of neglect that spans all circumstances (Horwath, 2013), because neglect is often a reflection of the cultural and community norms in which parenting and care are understood (individually, culturally, organisationally, and professionally). In addition to this, we cannot overlook the impact of individuals' values and beliefs. This extra layer is comprised of our individual experiences of being parented, and/or our own practices of caring for children ourselves. It is important to be aware of these different layers of perceptions as they are likely to inform practice-based decisions at individual, team or managerial levels, such as rationalising an assessment, instigating a child protection investigation, intervening in family life, or making the decision to allocate often scarce resources to a particular child(ren) to implement support for the household.

Basic needs

In the following table, Beesley (2011, p.35) sets out some signs that may help practitioners recognise when a child's basic needs may be unmet (sources of suggested evidence in italics).

Infants

Low birth weight, weight faltering *(centile charts, health and midwifery records)*

Withdrawal from drugs at birth; at risk from blood-borne viruses *(health records)*

Delay in physical development *(growth charts, health visitor records)*

Lack of bonding and early attachment *(observations, midwifery and health visitor records)*

Repetitive, self-soothing movements *(observations, reports from caregivers)*

Physical signs such as bruises, burns from being left in dirty nappies too long, lesions that have become infected *(observation, health records)*

Pre-school and school age

Delay in physical growth and development *(health, early years and education records)*

Delay in cognitive, speech and language development *(health and education records)*

Behavioural disturbance – excessive aggression, withdrawal, non-compliance, control *(observations, caregiver reports, reports from school)*

Anxious, insecure attachments to primary caregivers *(observations, attachment checklists, caregiver reports, child reports)*

Health problems, including hearing and sight difficulties *(school health)*

Wetting and soiling *(school health reports)*

Poor hygiene, smelly and dirty *(observation, reports from school, neighbours, family members)*

Inappropriate and unsuitable clothing *(observation, reports from school and others)*

Excessive appetite *(reports from school, caregivers, and others)*

Self-harm *(reports from school, health, caregiver, child observation, self)*

Poor or non-school attendance or attending school without proper equipment and clothing *(education records)*

Parents do not attend school events *(school records)*

Poor academic progress *(school reports)*

Lack of evidence of toys *(observation and questioning)*

Child not allowed to play outdoors *(child and caregiver reports)*

UNDERSTANDING CHILD NEGLECT

Difficulty in forming and keeping relationships with peers *(observation, reports from caregivers, school, child)*

Adolescents – those signs above plus those below

Anti-social behaviour *(reports from school, community, police)*

Drug and alcohol use *(observation, reports from caregivers, school, police and others)*

Being described as "beyond control" *(reports from caregivers, school and others)*

Going missing, running away *(reports from school, police, caregivers, young person)*

PERSONAL AND PROFESSIONAL INFLUENCES

There is no doubt that our individual experiences of childhood mould who we are and the way in which we approach our own parenting or caring roles. A person's experiences of how they have been parented and how they parent themselves will be unique: some will have grown up in loving and stable homes, whilst others may have suffered trauma, neglect or abuse in various forms (Beesley, 2011). It is important to acknowledge that as individuals, and therefore as individual practitioners, some people will not have experienced going without material goods at all, having had all their basic needs met in full, whilst others may have grown up in significant poverty or hardship and had to live with hunger or inadequate care. These experiences shape our understanding of how we perceive parenting and may impact on what we perceive to be "good enough" care for a child. This point is illustrated in the quote below from a member of school staff who refers to using her personal experiences of parenting to guide her perceptions of child maltreatment in a professional environment:

> *Yes, I had a good awareness of abuse and neglect...I felt prepared for the role – being a mum makes a big difference.*

> (School administrator, primary school)

7

As a social worker, I reflect on my own experiences of living in a neglectful home. Now knowing that this [childhood neglect] was the case, I have to be mindful of how this impacts upon my own practice. When we enter homes which have similarity to experiences in our own upbringings, this can influence how we judge the risk presented to the child – I could think, 'Well, after all, this was my experience, and I'm OK!' It can also take the other turn, of an overtly increased threshold decision, where potentially I make risk-adverse decisions. It is critical to be mindful of our own experiences when we are out on the frontline supporting children, we need to have the space to reflect to understand the impact of our own identities, for ourselves and how this may influence our practice with children.

When going into family homes, it is common to find poor housing conditions, poverty, children experiencing barriers to education or non-attendance at school, poor parental mental health and/or drug misuse. I have met many children in these environments and every time I am mindful of needing to ensure that my personal and professional boundaries are not blurred. When I am asked why I do the role I do, it is in part due to my own experiences: I want to support families with these challenges to see things can change. But to do this it must be with my professional lens. That is not to disregard my personal experiences – these enable me to bring a humanistic aspect to the way in which I practice, with empathy and understanding.

(Juanita Scallan, independent social worker)

In addition to our personal influences, professional knowledge frameworks and organisational cultures can also contribute to the way we conceptualise whether care is considered "good enough" or not. For example, the perceptions and views of colleagues or managers and the operational categories used by your organisation to define child neglect will significantly impact on your perspectives. The narrower operational category for neglect will be used as a threshold for intervention and the provision of support services and access to resources. Members of the same team or organisation, or multi-agency group, may not agree on what necessitates adequate care, placing emphasis on different elements of care and parenting (Horwath, 2013).

The potential for becoming desensitised to neglect is also important to consider. For practitioners who frequently come into contact with children or families where chronic neglect is present, it may mean that it becomes more difficult to see poor or inadequate standards of parenting as neglectful – when all of the families living in the neighbourhood, and/or all of the children on their caseloads are living in or experiencing similar environments (Beesley, 2011).

It is therefore important to reflect on your experiences of your own caregiving and receiving – to inform your understandings for practice. Beesley (2011) poses the following set of questions to help practitioners to consider this. This activity can be undertaken individually, in supervision, or with a colleague to explore your feelings, perceptions and uncertainties.

- What does "parenting capacity" mean to me?

- Does it mean the same to my colleagues?

- Where does my understanding of "good enough" parenting come from?

- What is my understanding of what children need from family life?

- What does the term "child neglect" mean to me?

- How will I know neglect when I see it?

(Beesley, 2011, p.6)

DIVERSITY AND CULTURE

In addition to the factors mentioned above, your own ethnicity, culture, class, (dis)ability and gender can all contribute to your relationships with families, and the beliefs, values and prejudices that you may hold about different societal groups. These beliefs may influence conceptions of child neglect and what you perceive to be "good enough" parenting in a range of different contexts. Although children from black and minority ethnic backgrounds in the UK are disproportionately represented in the child protection system (Turney, 2016), this does not mean that black and minority ethnic parents or carers maltreat their children more, or that they have more disciplinary parenting approaches.

Whilst there is a lack of research exploring black families' experiences within the child protection system where neglect is a concern, being from a black or minority ethnic group is associated with experiencing high levels of poverty, unemployment, inadequate housing (Beesley, 2011) and experiences of social injustice, oppression or inequalities, as recently highlighted by the Covid-19 pandemic in 2020/21 (Suleman *et al*, 2021). The interrelated relationship between neglect and poverty is considered in more detail in Chapter 4. Turney (2016) suggests the intersectionality of these issues can make black families more vulnerable as well as increasingly visible to statutory involvement in family life. It is important to be sensitive to cultural or class differences when supporting children and families. However, it is essential that the worry of imposing your own values and beliefs does not inadvertently blur your vision to the signs or indicators of neglect that may be presented. Finding ways to understand and identify neglectful parenting and care within your assessments, and doing so in a considered and culturally appropriate way that understands cultural dynamics and influences, should be central to practice (Turney, 2016).

> The following questions, adapted from Dalzell and Sawyer's "cultural review" exercise, may be useful in helping you to reflect on your own knowledge and prejudices.
>
> 1. What do I know about individuals and families with this particular cultural background or life experience?
>
> 2. Where does my knowledge come from?
>
> 3. What prejudices [or assumptions] may I hold [positive or negative]?
>
> 4. What might surprise me about this family and why would it be a surprise?
>
> 5. How might this parent/child/family perceive me?
>
> 6. What impact might my preconceptions have on the family's life?
>
> 7. What individual or organisational norms do I take with me?
>
> (Adapted from Dalzell and Sawyer, 2016, p. 37)

WHY IS NEGLECT SO CHALLENGING FOR PRACTICE?

Neglect is a chronic and pervasive public health issue, with 1 in 10 children aged 11–17 having experienced neglect at some point in their lives (NSPCC, 2021a). Neglect remains the most prevalent form of maltreatment, being identified for half of all children on child protection plans or on the child protection register in the UK (NSPCC, 2022a). However, neglect as a form of child maltreatment can be said to have lacked attention compared to other forms of abuse. This could be because it continues to be considered less serious than other forms of maltreatment (Allnock, 2016), is often cumulative and not always immediately observable in all its forms (Sharley, 2018). Because neglect is rarely based on a specific incident and has no single cause (Holland *et al*, 2013; NSPCC, 2015a and b), it is not uncommon for professionals to wait for a trigger event (such as an instance of physical abuse) to provide evidence that adds weight to a referral to statutory services where neglect has in fact been a longstanding concern (Sharley, 2018). This is a substantial issue for practice, which leaves children exposed to the impact of ongoing neglect that will have significant and varied consequences throughout the individual's lifespan (Allnock, 2016).

For most practitioners, **physical neglect** is probably the most familiar type of neglect (Horwath, 2007). Its visible nature means that the effects of physical neglect can be easier for professionals to see (Sharley, 2019). Physical neglect can be observed in the child's appearance and seen in the manifestation of an unhygienic or inadequate living environment. It may appear as dirty clothing or tidemarks on a child's skin, the smell of body odour, dirt and faeces due to poor hygiene, and poor-fitting or insufficient clothing for the child's age or climate. Staff in schools may observe the absence of food in packed-lunch boxes, or children who are hungry. Home conditions (perhaps less immediately detectable for practitioners who do not undertake home visits), may include damp or unheated houses, the absence of electricity, water, heating, food or toiletries, and inadequate safety guards for home appliances, fires or stairs (Sharley, 2018).

In addition to physical neglect, there are a number of different types of neglect acknowledged within the literature (Horwath, 2007; Daniel *et al*, 2011; Farmer and Lutman, 2012); these include:

- medical neglect;
- nutritional neglect;
- emotional neglect;
- educational neglect; and
- lack of appropriate supervision or guidance.

Medical neglect can refer to denying or diminishing a child's illness or health needs, including dental and optical care, speech and language therapy, and failing to seek necessary medical attention or treatments (Erterm *et al*, 2002). Children with complex needs are increasingly vulnerable to medical neglect as they can require frequent or intensive support from their parent or carer for a wide range of health needs (Sullivan and Knutson, 2000).

Nutritional neglect can occur when a child or young person is not provided with adequate food or nutrition for growth (Hobbs and Wynne, 2002) or, on the contrary, can relate to obesity due to unhealthy diet and lack of exercise.

Emotional neglect is associated with either hostile or indifferent parent or carer behaviours that damage a child's emotional wellbeing, value or self-worth. Emotional neglect often takes the form of a lack of parental interaction, stimulation and the absence of emotional warmth and care.

This in turn, can fail to allow a child to develop a sense of belonging and positive self-identity (Horwath, 2007).

Aside from the school's duties and responsibilities as educators, **educational neglect** can also take place when a parent or carer fails to ensure that a child has access to an appropriate education. Aside from persistent lateness to or absences from school, educational neglect can also more broadly include aspects of carers not supporting the child's learning and development, not providing sufficient stimulation, not taking an interest in the child's education, not identifying their educational or learning needs, and not engaging with their child's learning through parents' consultation evenings and events.

These types of neglect are more difficult to evidence compared to *seeing* the physical indicators mentioned earlier in this chapter. They may also be a result of specific timing, or a parent's or carer's intention, or lack of intention, in terms of how they are experienced by a child (Beesley, 2011). For example, a child may not be taken to the GP when they are in need of medical care, or a parent or carer may not attend parents' evenings at the school, meaning they do not appropriately respond to a child's basic emotional or physical needs at a specific point in time. Making a judgement about whether neglect has occurred or not is a challenge for practice – it is important to consider the following aspects:

- the practitioner's understanding of children's basic needs;

- the age and developmental stage of the child;

- the parents' or caregivers' intention;

- whether parents/carers have had reasonable access to resources to meet a child's basic needs satisfactorily (Horwath, 2007);

- whether neglect is a one-off incident or episodic and chronic.

CHILDREN AND YOUNG PEOPLE'S UNDERSTANDINGS

Children and young people can have different understandings of what constitutes neglect, perhaps in contrast to the views and understandings of practitioners. There is limited research on children and young peoples' experiences of neglect. This could be connected to the practical difficulties in gaining access to recruit children as participants (McLeod, 2007; Farmer and Lutman, 2012), or the fact that research with children can require more time, energy and resources (Gorin, 2016) than that with adults. Sensitive research also has the potential to cause distress to minors, many of whom are already vulnerable and are either being protected by statutory services or are in need of protection (Sharley, 2018). This is in addition to the conceptual complexity and multifaceted nature of neglect discussed earlier in this chapter, and holds importance for practice as children and young people's views and perceptions of how they are parented and what they need can vary significantly from the perspectives of the adults who are parenting them, and the professionals who may be offering support to both.

In Radford *et al*'s (2011) *Child Safety and Victimisation Survey*, undertaken in the UK, the views of over 3,000 children and young people aged 11-24 years old were gathered. The study, the largest to provide robust evidence on young people's views on neglect, reported that 10 per cent of children aged 11–17 had experienced "severe" neglect, including significant emotional neglect, lack of supervision or care which would place them at risk, or neglect which was defined as abusive or criminal.

The study *Action on Neglect* (Daniel *et al*, 2014, p. 277) explored ways in which children who are neglected are helped. It provided new and powerful perceptions of neglect from a young people's group, offering insights into what children and young people felt like when they were neglected. Children defined neglect as being 'not enough love', 'having no interest in me', 'having to look after siblings', 'you end up doing your parents' job', 'the responsibility is passed to you', and insightfully, 'when parents neglect themselves'. Key messages from the study emphasised that children and young people believe that spoken words are not sufficient to ameliorate parents' or carers' responsibility for acts of practical care – 'love is a doing word'.

> *...its one thing to say they love you [parents] but they have to show it.*

(Young person, in Daniel *et al*, 2014, p. 277)

Aside from differing perceptions between children/young people and their parents or carers, some children and young people may feel that they will not be believed by practitioners if they choose to disclose experiences of neglect (Tucker, 2011). This is an important point that can be an added barrier as children and young people may feel that telling someone could make their situation worse. Children and young people who have experienced neglect can be "touch-hungry" with adults, striving for physical contact or affection, such as from a teacher or staff member at school (Erikson *et al*, 1989) (the concept of touch is explored in more detail in Chapter 9). It is also important to be mindful that experiencing neglect (rather than any other form of maltreatment) is particularly likely to wear away a child or young person's confidence, their ability to identify the need for help, and their ability to seek support from someone (Jobe and Gorin, 2013; Daniel *et al*, 2014). This means that children who are living with neglect may be less able (than others) to seek the support they are in fact most in need of receiving. Further, children and young people are more likely to display secondary signs of needing help (as opposed to disclosing experiences of neglect), such as withdrawing in the classroom or displaying challenging behaviours, rather than asking professionals for help directly (Gorin, 2004). It is not uncommon for children who are living with neglect to be excluded for what is perceived as "behavioural issues", or because they are frequently late to school, or have high levels of absence (Harford, 2018). This in turn increases their vulnerability and consequently makes children less visible to professionals in schools, and health-based universal services, where they would ordinarily be seen by a range of adults on a regular basis (Sharley, 2020).

RESPONDING TO A DISCLOSURE

There can be many reasons why a child or young person may not feel able to tell someone that they have experienced or are living with neglect. This may be because they do not recognise the care they are receiving as being neglectful; they love and care for their parent or caregiver; they may not feel able to trust someone enough to tell them; they are too worn down; they are worried about the consequences for the person responsible; they have not been directly asked about it; or they are worried that as a result things may become worse (NSPCC, 2022a).

What to say to a child and how to respond

The following tips on how to respond to a disclosure may be useful to consider.

1. **Listen carefully**	Be patient and focus on what you are being told. Try not to express your own views and feelings. If you appear shocked or as if you do not believe the child, it could make them stop talking and take back what they have said.
2. **Give them the tools to talk**	If they are struggling to talk to you, use alternative methods of communication to help them express their thoughts and feelings.
3. **Let them know they've done nothing wrong**	Reassurance can make a big impact, particularly if they have kept the information secret for a long time.
4. **Tell them it's not their fault**	Neglect is never a child's fault, so it is important to ensure they hear and know this.

5. **Say you'll take them seriously**	They may have kept the neglect secret as they thought they would not be believed. Say they can trust you and you will listen and support them.
6. **Don't confront the alleged abuser**	Confronting the alleged abuser could make the situation worse for the child.
7. **Explain what you will do next**	Take time to ensure you explain what will happen next in an age-appropriate way.
8. **Report what the child has told you as soon as possible**	As soon as you have been told, take action and report the neglect to children's services.

(Taken from NSPCC website, 2022a)

WHAT LESSONS HAVE WE LEARNED?

Child safeguarding practice reviews in England (previously called serious case reviews) and child practice reviews in Wales take place when a child dies or is seriously harmed, and there is a concern that abuse and/or neglect are known factors. The purpose of these reviews is to identify ways that practice locally and nationally can be improved to safeguard children more effectively, to avoid or prevent similar instances happening again (NSPCC, 2022a). These reviews provide valuable opportunities for all professionals working with children, with the aim of supporting better practice and improving policies. Sadly, neglect is a recurrent theme in reviews, which make the overview analyses and reports invaluable in offering us important messages for practice (Beesley, 2011).

Historic and recurrent themes

Beesley (2011, p. 21) suggests that cases of neglect are complex and often include a multiplicity of factors – such as social and economic deprivation combined with parental difficulties. Neglect is also associated with domestic abuse, mental health difficulties and substance misuse, commonly referred to as the "toxic trio" (Coordinated Action Against Domestic Abuse (CAADA), 2014) (see Chapter 5), and it is not uncommon for neglect to occur across familial generations. There are a number of themes that have emerged and continue to emerge in local and national practice reviews that provide a useful checklist for practitioners.

- Loss of focus on the child, due to focus on the adults' needs.

WORKING WITH CHILDREN WHO HAVE EXPERIENCED NEGLECT

- Lack of overview or reflection on the patterns in the case.

- Poor assessment and analysis.

- Not recognising indicators of risk of harm from chronic neglect

- Not acting on assessment, or loss of momentum on parental progress.

- Over-optimism about parental capacity in difficult circumstances.

- Poor information sharing, recording, management, supervision and training.

Neglect and serious case reviews

Brandon *et al*'s (2020) analysis of serious case reviews, *Complexity and Challenge: A triennial analysis of SCRs 2014–2017*, rehearses many of the lessons and themes also identified in past studies, only emphasising the challenging and complex nature of neglect for practice. The analysis examined 368 child safeguarding practice reviews in England, with more detailed analysis of 278 cases. Neglect featured in nearly three-quarters of the reviews (74.8%). Neglect is consistently the most common category of abuse for children on a child protection plan in England – and was the category of abuse in over half of the children who were subject to a child protection plan at the time of, or prior to, the incident leading to the review. In these reviews, neglect typically included poor dental hygiene and untreated dental needs, incomplete vaccinations due to missed routine health care appointments, poor school attendance, and developmental delays due to lack of stimulation (p. 41). The analysis found three overarching issues: poverty; the complex and cumulative nature of neglect; and the invisibility of some children and young people to the system. These aspects are explored in more depth in Chapter 4 on identifying neglect, and Chapter 5 on Adverse Childhood Experiences.

PRACTITIONER TIPS

- Be self-aware – we know our histories and how these can impact practice, we need to have the ability not to influence our practice.

- Be authentic and consider your professional boundaries in your practice.

- Utilise supervision – this is imperative, the reflective space to consider, understand and ensure objectivity.

- Engage in group supervision with colleagues, gain various perspectives; this will help identify the impact of your own personal and professional experiences and your understanding of risk.

- Draw on an evidence base; be sure your decisions are based in evidence, not sweeping judgements.

- Develop relationships with children and their parents/carers; with experience, we become effective in empathy and understanding. This can be really useful in breaking down barriers and providing positive interventions.

FURTHER READING AND RESOURCES

Websites

NSPCC (2022) *Protecting Children from Radicalisation*, available at: https://bit.ly/3ILT1Yt

Practice and policy briefings

Baynes P (2020) *Life Story Work: Why does it matter?*, available at: https://bit.ly/3H0n2mc

Daniel B, Burgess C, Whitfield E, Derbyshire D and Taylor J (2014) *Action on Neglect: A resource pack*, available at: https://bit.ly/3X14asN

Research

Brandon M, Sidebotham P, Belderson P, Cleaver H, Dickens J, Garstang J, Harris J, Sorensen P and Wate R (2020) *Complexity and Challenge: A triennial analysis of serious case reviews 2014–2017*, available at https://bit.ly/3ZLRJmD

Chapter 2
Legislation and policy

Julie Doughty, Cardiff University School of Law and Politics

INTRODUCTION

This chapter outlines the legal context of child neglect for social work practitioners. It explains where to find the powers and duties that local authorities and agencies have so that they can work with, assess, support and protect children from neglect. It also covers the existing policies and guidance to be followed.

Very serious cases of child neglect can be prosecuted in the criminal justice system, under the Children and Young Persons Act 1933. The grounds for a criminal offence are where a child under 16 has been neglected in a way likely to cause injury to their health, or the parent/carer has failed to provide them with adequate food, clothing, medical aid or a place to live. This chapter does not include aspects of criminal law, but explains child and family law, as it affects social work practice.

The chapter is structured as follows:

- children in need;
- child protection;
- court proceedings;
- placement;
- support.

In each section, the relevant legislation is set out, followed by current policies and guidance. References cited apply to both England and Wales, except where indicated. In England, policy responsibility for children's services lies with the Department for Education (DfE); in Wales, with Welsh Government. The major difference between the law of England and Wales is that duties to assess and support children in need are now found in separate legislation. However, this divergence does not lead to a different approach to good practice. It is also important to keep human rights principles in mind, including Article 8 of the European Convention on Human Rights, the right to respect for family life, and the UN Convention on the Rights of the Child, especially Article 9, the child's right not be separated from their parents unless necessary in their best interests because of abuse or neglect. Brief summaries of the corresponding legislation and policy in Northern Ireland and Scotland are included later in this chapter.

The Children Act 1989 set out local authority powers and duties to support children in need and their families in Part III (ss.17–30). These sections have been repealed in Wales and replaced by Part VI (ss.74–125) of the Social Services and Well-being (Wales) Act 2014. This will be explained in subsequent sections. Provisions for child protection and court proceedings (in Parts V and IV respectively) still apply in both England and Wales. Some regulations and statutory guidance are different, and these will be highlighted. ('Statutory guidance' is guidance issued by Government that should always be followed unless circumstances justify a departure from it.)

At the time of writing, there is some discussion about outcomes of the Independent Review of Children's Social Care in England (MacAlister, 2022) and whether statutory duties to support children in need and to comply with child protection procedures may be restructured. The chapter is based on the original holistic ethos of the Children Act 1989, under which these duties arise across a spectrum of meeting children's needs.

SUPPORTING CHILDREN WHO ARE AT RISK OF NEGLECT

Children in need

In England, there is a general duty under s.17 of the Children Act 1989 to safeguard and promote the welfare of children in need in the local authority's area, and to promote their upbringing by their family, by providing a range of services. A child in need is defined in s.17(10) as a child who (a) needs services to achieve or maintain a reasonable standard of health or development, or (b) needs services to prevent impairment to their health, or (c) is disabled. A list of specific duties in Part 1 of Schedule 2 of the Act includes, at paragraph 4, a duty to take reasonable steps to provide services to prevent children from suffering ill-treatment or neglect. Ill treatment is defined, but as there is no definition in the Act of neglect, it just has an ordinary meaning, as explored throughout this book. There are some definitions in the statutory guidance, referred to below.

Case law has, however, interpreted the s.17 duty as merely a general one, with no specific targeted duty toward an individual child, because of limited local authority resources (*R (G) v London Borough of Barnet; R (W) v London Borough of Lambeth* [2003] UKHL 57). This means that a local authority is legally allowed to spend public money on services intended to prevent or lessen child neglect in the area, but is not under a legal duty to alleviate the circumstances that are causing an individual child to be at risk of neglect. A child with disabilities may, however, have access to individual services through the Chronically Sick and Disabled Persons Act 1970, where s.2 places a specific duty on a local authority to provide services to meet the assessed needs of children with disabilities. The list of types of services in this Act is wide, including personal care and home adaptations that would support a parent who might otherwise be struggling to adequately care for the child.

In Wales, s.17 was repealed in 2016 and replaced by new legislation. A child who appears to need care and support will be assessed under Part 3 of the Social Services and Well-being (Wales) Act 2014. If the assessment concludes that services are needed to prevent neglect or reduce its impact, these will be planned under Part 4 of the Act in accordance with eligibility criteria. Parts 3 and 4 are supported by regulations, statutory guidance and codes of practice (all available on the Social Care Wales website). The Wales Act includes a brief definition of neglect as: a failure to meet a person's basic physical, emotional, social or psychological needs, which is likely to result in an impairment of the person's well-being (for example, an impairment of the person's health or, in the case of a child, an impairment of the child's development) (s.197).

Section 17 in England is not accompanied by its own separate regulations or statutory guidance, but comes within the *Working Together* guidance (explained below). While it may appear problematic to find guidance on family support as part of safeguarding guidance, s.17 is envisaged as part of "early help" to prevent abuse and neglect. Local authorities in England do not apply specific eligibility criteria to s.17 services, but are required to publish a threshold document, which sets out the local criteria for action in a way that is transparent, accessible and easily understood (para 16). Local authorities, with their partner agencies, are also required to develop and publish local protocols for assessment that set out clear arrangements for how cases will be managed once a child is referred into children's social care and be consistent with the requirements of *Working Together* (para 46).

Accommodating children at risk of suffering neglect

Part III of the Children Act 1989, about family support, also contains a duty under s.20 to accommodate and maintain a child whose parents cannot do so. In Wales, this duty is found in s.76 of the Social Services and Well-being (Wales) Act 2014. The wording in the provisions for 'looked-after children' is almost identical in both Acts. Children in voluntary care under s.20/s.76 are commonly known as looked after, although these duties also apply to children on care orders (as explained below). The s.20/s.76 voluntary provisions should not be used where a child is at risk of serious harm, because they depend on parental consent that can be withdrawn at any time. Best practice guidance on the use of s.20/s.76 has been published by the Public Law Working Group (2021).

Duties toward children looked after are set out in detail in regulations: the *Care Planning, Placement and Case Review Regulations 2010* in England, and the *Care Planning, Placement and Case Review (Wales) Regulations 2015*. Statutory guidance is contained in *Children Act 1989 Guidance and Regulations Volume 2: Care Planning, Placement and Case Review 2010* and, in Wales, the *Part 6 Code of Practice.*

CHILD PROTECTION AND NEGLECT

Child protection procedures

Where a local authority has reasonable cause to suspect that a child in their area is suffering, or is likely to suffer, significant harm, they must undertake an investigation under s.47 of the Children Act 1989. 'Harm' means ill-treatment or the impairment of the child's development (s.31(9)). 'Significant' is discussed below, with regard to care orders.

Child protection procedures for England are set out in *Working Together to Safeguard Children* (2018). In *Working Together*, there is little reference to neglect as such, because the terminology throughout refers to 'abuse and neglect', making it clear that the impact of neglect is no less serious than other types of abuse. Neglect is defined separately in a glossary as:

> *The persistent failure to meet a child's basic physical and/or psychological needs, likely to result in the serious impairment of the child's health or development. Neglect may occur during pregnancy as a result of maternal substance abuse. Once a child is born, neglect may involve a parent or carer failing to:*
>
> a. *provide adequate food, clothing and shelter (including exclusion from home or abandonment)*
>
> b. *protect a child from physical and emotional harm or danger*
>
> c. *ensure adequate supervision (including the use of inadequate care-givers)*
>
> d. *ensure access to appropriate medical care or treatment*

It may also include neglect of, or unresponsiveness to, a child's basic emotional needs (p. 108).

The Welsh statutory guidance is found in *Working Together to Safeguard People Volume 5.* This is supported by the All Wales Safeguarding Procedures, in which child neglect is defined as:

The failure to meet a child's basic and essential needs including physical, emotional and medical needs. It can include a failure to provide adequate food, clothing and shelter, failure to protect a child from physical and emotional harm and failure to provide adequate medical care or treatment. It can occur during pregnancy as a result of maternal substance abuse. It can also occur before a child is born where a parent fails to prepare appropriately for the child's birth, fails to seek ante-natal care, and/or engages in behaviours that place the baby at risk. Neglect can take different forms, ranging from obvious physical signs such as being inadequately clothed to young children being left alone in their home or on the streets for long periods of time. Children may lack parental support to go to school, miss health appointments, and be ignored when distressed.

Note that, as well as the definition in the All Wales Procedures being written in more accessible language than *Working Together*, this builds on the definition in the Social Services and Well-being (Wales) Act 2014 in that it does not refer to "persistent" failure to meet a child's needs. The examples given are, however, illustrative of a pattern of neglect. In order to prove harmful neglect in court proceedings in England, the evidential burden on the local authority may be greater, to satisfy the court the harm is persistent. However, this variation in wording does not suggest that practice should differ between England and Wales – rather that the effect on the child should be the focus, not quantifying what might add up to "persistent".

The All Wales Procedures resource includes an All Wales Practice Guide, *Safeguarding Children from Neglect*, which is a comprehensive guide to the underlying principles, different types of neglect, and the evidence base. Although these procedures and guides do not have the status of statutory guidance, they were produced collaboratively and are followed by local authorities and other relevant agencies.

Child practice reviews (CPRs)

Formerly known as serious case reviews, these are conducted when a child dies or is seriously harmed as a result of abuse or neglect, in order to identify ways that professionals and organisations can improve the way they work together to safeguard children and prevent similar incidents from occurring. CPRs in England are subject to the *Working Together* guidance (above). In Wales, the criteria for CPRs are laid down in the Safeguarding Boards (Functions and Procedures) (Wales) Regulations 2015 and statutory guidance is contained in *Working Together to Safeguard People Volume 2: Child Practice Reviews.*

A summary published by the NSPCC of CPRs that featured neglect between 2003 and 2011 found that:

- *Neglect was much more prevalent in serious case reviews than had previously been understood (identified in 60 per cent of 139 reviews from 2009–2011).*

- *Neglect can be life threatening and needs to be treated with as much urgency as other categories of maltreatment.*

- *Neglect with the most serious outcomes is not confined to the youngest children, and occurs across all ages.*

- *The possibility that in a very small minority of cases neglect will be fatal, or cause grave harm, should be part of a practitioner's mindset.*

- *Practitioners, managers, policy-makers and decision-makers should be discouraged from minimising or downgrading the harm that can come from neglect and from allowing neglect cases to drift.*

- *The key aim for practitioners working with neglect was to ensure a healthy living environment and healthy relationships for children.*

- *Prevention and early access to help and support for children and their families were crucial, but so too was later stage help for older children who live with the consequences of longstanding neglect.*

(Brandon *et al*, 2013)

The NSPCC holds a searchable repository of CPRs that indicates that in the first six months of 2022, 28 reviews featured neglect. In a report from the Child Practice Review Panel on incidents reported in 2020, 12 per cent of cases of non-fatal serious harm were caused by neglect, second to the number (38%) caused by physical abuse. However, about one-third of all notifications mentioned neglect as an underlying feature.

A thematic analysis of 20 CPRs in Wales from 2014–2019 found that in four of these reviews, the use of inconsistent language across agencies had partly led to adverse outcomes for children. Loose terminology regarding home conditions in cases of neglect could hinder understanding of risk and impact on court processes, because of poor or inconsistent evidence (Rees *et al*, 2021b).

COURT PROCEEDINGS

In all decisions made by a court under the Children Act 1989, the child's welfare is its paramount consideration (s.1).

Care orders

Where social work assessments conclude that there is a likelihood of significant harm attributable to abuse or neglect, the local authority has a duty to apply for a care order under s.31 of the Children Act 1989. Section 31 includes what have become known as "threshold criteria", which have to be proved for the court to make a care order. "Significant" harm regarding child development means as compared with a similar child (s.31(10)). As Lady Hale explained in a Supreme Court judgement, "ill treatment" generally involves some active conduct but "impairment" can also result from neglecting the child's needs for food, warmth, shelter, love, education and health care. In the same case, Lord Wilson confirmed that courts should not attempt to define "significant", but that each case turns on its own facts (*Re B (A Child) (Care Proceedings) (Appeal)* [2013] UKSC 13. In *Re B*, the court discussed some famous words by Mr Justice Hedley in an earlier case, that:

> *...society must be willing to tolerate very diverse standards of parenting, including the eccentric, the barely adequate and the inconsistent... Significant harm is fact specific and must retain the breadth of meaning that human fallibility may require of it...it is clear that it must be something unusual; at least something more than the commonplace human failure or inadequacy.*

> (*Re L (Threshold Criteria)* [2006] EWCC 2 (Fam) at para 50)

Specific evidence linking the facts in each case to the assessment of the impact on the child and the necessity for a care order is therefore required (see also *Re A*, below).

Under a care order, the child becomes looked after but, unlike s.20/s.76, here the local authority shares parental responsibility with the parent/s and will direct where the child should live. Before applying for a care order, the local authority follows the Public Law Outline Pre-Proceedings process as set out in statutory guidance, *Court Orders and Pre-Proceedings for Local Authorities* (DfE, 2014). The key stages in pre-proceedings are sending a letter to the parents, advising them that the local authority is considering starting care proceedings, and inviting them to a meeting accompanied by a lawyer, to discuss what they could do to prevent this. At the meeting, the local authority explains what assessments it intends to do in the pre-proceedings stage, and any requirements of the parents. This may be recorded in a written agreement or statement of expectations. The pre-proceedings letter enables parents to apply for legal aid to obtain legal representation. In cases of neglect, the record of how the parents need to demonstrate change needs to be very clear.

If the application for a care order goes ahead, this is accompanied by a social work chronology, a social work statement, the current assessments, and a care plan. The local authority lawyer will draft a threshold document based on this evidence. In a case heard in 2015, the court emphasised the need to establish the link between facts relied upon in a threshold document and the conclusion that the child has suffered, or is at risk of suffering, significant harm. Sometimes the link will be obvious, if the facts proved establish physical harm. The link may be less obvious where the allegation is that the child is at risk of suffering emotional harm or, as in this case, was at risk of suffering neglect. A substantial part of the local authority's case here was that the father 'lacked honesty', 'minimised matters of importance' and was 'immature and lacks insight'. The court found that this line of evidence did not naturally feed through into a conclusion that the child was at risk of neglect. It was emphasised that the local authority's evidence and submissions must set out the argument and explain explicitly why it is said that, in the particular case, the conclusion indeed follows from the facts (*Re A (A Child)* [2015] EWFC 11).

The initial application to court will be for an interim care order (ICO). Parents may at this stage agree s.20/s.76 arrangements while the proceedings are ongoing, or the child may remain at home under an interim order. If neither of these arrangements can keep the child safe, and the local authority is therefore applying to remove the child under the ICO, the immediate risk to the child must be clearly presented in evidence. As the Court of Appeal explained in a judgement in 2020, an interim order is sought at a stage when the evidence is incomplete and should only be made with regard to matters that cannot await the final hearing. Removal of a child at an interim stage is 'a particularly sharp interference' with human rights and an order will only be justified where it is both necessary and proportionate. A plan for immediate separation will only be agreed by the court 'where the child's physical safety or psychological or emotional welfare demands it and where the length and likely consequences of the separation are a proportionate response to the risks that would arise if it did not occur'. The local authority should inform the court of any options and available resources that could avoid the need for separation at an interim stage (*Re C (A Child: Interim Separation)* [2020] EWCA Civ 257).

In a report on a study by Masson and colleagues on public law reforms, they described the courts' view of an ICO with removal as a 'last resort' and observed that, in cases of neglect, courts may be unwilling to make an ICO or permit removal because the local authority has accepted the situation for so long, and removal would disrupt relationships or prejudge the main proceedings (Masson *et al*, 2019, p. 126). However, serious neglect was recognised as very damaging to children and the majority of care cases in their study did involve neglect. They found that the courts were generally satisfied that the threshold for significant harm in neglect cases was met, with very low proportions of cases being dismissed or ending without an order (Masson *et al*, 2019, p. 251).

If the threshold criteria are met but the parents are co-operating with agencies and demonstrating the capacity to change, a 12-month supervision order may be more proportionate than a care order.

Emergency protection orders and police powers

In urgent cases, where a child needs to be removed from their parents because of sudden or imminent harm, the local authority should apply for an emergency protection order (EPO), under which it will share parental responsibility for up to eight days. An EPO is not appropriate in a case of ongoing chronic neglect, unless there is a change in circumstances that creates a genuine emergency. Separation under an EPO is only to be contemplated if immediate separation is essential to secure the child's safety: 'imminent danger' must be 'actually established'. The evidence in support of the application must be full, detailed, precise and compelling (*X Council v B (Emergency Protection Order)* [2004] EWHC 2015).

In cases of long standing neglect that have reached the significant harm threshold, an application should be made for a care order in the usual way, although the pre-proceedings stage may need to be dispensed with in some circumstances (Practice Direction, para 3.1)

The police have powers under s.46 of the Children Act 1989 to remove a child from a dangerous situation for up to 72 hours and notify children's services. This action is appropriate where a young child is found alone, for example, or their parents are in circumstances that mean they cannot keep their children safe at that point in time.

Care plans

Further to the initial care plan supporting the application, a final care plan will subsequently be submitted to court that evaluates the options for the child's future if they cannot safely return to their parent/s, whether placed in foster care under the care order, or with extended family, or placement for adoption. The plan will explain how the child's needs that have arisen through neglect will be met by future support, for example, in catching up with education or medical care. The legal status of the placement will vary, according to whether the child is looked after, subject to a special guardianship order, or adopted. This means that the legal framework for support will also be different, although social work assessment of a child's needs arising from a history of neglect will focus on the support needed for the particular carers.

PLACEMENT AND SUPPORT IN FOSTERING, SPECIAL GUARDIANSHIP AND ADOPTION

Foster care

The majority of looked after children are placed with local authority foster carers. Parental responsibility is shared between the parent/s and the local authority but it is the local authority's duty to accommodate and maintain the child, as set out in ss.20–24 of the Children Act 1989 (Social Services and Well-being (Wales) Act 2014, Part 6). There is detailed statutory guidance on care planning and reviews in *Children Act 1989 Guidance and Regulations Volume 2: Care Planning, Placement and Case Review 2010* and, in Wales, the *Part 6 Code*.

Kinship care

If kinship (family and friends) carers are approved as foster carers, the same planning and review legal framework applies as above. Extra *Family and Friends Care: Statutory guidance for local authorities* (2011) also applies in England. The same rates of fostering allowances should be paid to kinship foster carers as those paid to unrelated foster carers (*R (X) v Tower Hamlets LBC* 2013 EWHC (Admin)). Where kinship carers become special guardians, a different framework applies because the child is not looked after.

Special guardianship

Increasing numbers of children are subject to special guardianship orders, the numbers of which now exceed adoption orders being made. Special guardians share parental responsibility with the parents but exercise this exclusively. They often need considerable support, especially with contact arrangements (Hunt, 2021). Support services are provided under s.14F of the Children Act 1989, including counselling, advice and information services. Prospective special guardians can request an assessment to include financial support. The regulations and guidance are the *Special Guardianship Regulations 2005* and statutory guidance issued in 2016 in England, and *Special Guardianship Regulations (Wales) 2005* and *Code of Practice*, issued in 2018. A recent case on financial support confirmed that it is unlawful for a local authority to depart from guidance on rates of allowances without giving reasons for doing so (*R (Becker) v Plymouth City Council* [2022] EWHC 1885 (Admin)).

Adoption

Where children are suffering from the effects of neglect, adoptive families may request an assessment for support services under s.4 of the Adoption and Children Act 2002. Regulations give more details of the types of services that may be provided, including financial support, help with contact, therapy, and peer support groups. These are the *Adoption Support Services Regulations 2005* and *Adoption Support Services Regulations (Wales) 2005*. In England, guidance on support is found in Chapter 9 of *Statutory Guidance on Adoption 2013*. It is of course essential for the child's needs to be fully assessed when the adoption decision-maker concludes that a placement order should be applied for. However, support needs for adopted children can often emerge some years later.

LAW AND POLICY IN NORTHERN IRELAND

Principles of child protection in Northern Ireland are similar to England and Wales, with regard to the concepts of children in need of support and intervention where there is risk of significant harm. State responsibilities for children's welfare are, however, organised in a different type of structure, through regional health and social care trusts, rather than local authorities. The relevant legislation is the Children (Northern Ireland) Order 1995. Safeguarding policy is contained in *Co-operating to Safeguard Children and Young People in Northern Ireland* (Department of Health, 2017). Neglect is defined as 'failure to provide for a child's basic needs, whether it be adequate food, clothing, hygiene, supervision or shelter that is likely to result in the serious impairment of a child's health or development' (p. 14). Guidance on child protection procedures is contained in *Regional Core Child Protection Policies and Procedures for Northern Ireland* (Safeguarding Board for Northern Ireland, 2018). The evolution of policy and some divergences between the approach to child welfare and the tackling of neglect in Northern Ireland compared to other parts of the UK are discussed in Devany and McConville, 2016.

LAW AND POLICY IN SCOTLAND

The legal system in Scotland is entirely different to the rest of the UK, with court proceedings about child protection being conducted as children's hearings, a more community-based and less legalistic approach than that taken by the England and Wales family justice system. Legislation on public duties toward children is found in the Children (Scotland) Act 1995 and multi-disciplinary guidance in *National Child Protection Guidance for Scotland* (Scottish Government, 2021). This document states that neglect consists of persistent failure to meet a child's basic physical and/or psychological needs, which is likely to result in the serious impairment of the child's health or development. However, it adds that there can be single instances of neglectful behaviour that cause significant harm and that neglect can arise in the context of systemic stresses such as poverty, and is consequently an indicator of both support and protection needs (p. 13). This document contains considerably more detail on professional approaches to neglect (at pp. 142–145) than the guidance in the other jurisdictions. Scottish Government also published a series of reports on tackling child neglect in 2018; policy on neglect is currently evolving as part of the government's Improving Child Protection Programme.

DISCUSSION AND KEY MESSAGES

Legal obligations on local authorities to protect children from neglect extend from early family support and prevention through to seeking court intervention to providing services for children who suffer the effects of parental neglect throughout their childhood. UK child law is clear that children should be supported to be brought up by their own families when this is safe and that they should only be removed from their parents when this is necessary. This inevitably creates tensions in practice, when dealing with the complexities of family dynamics. Fundamental human rights include the right to respect for family life in Article 8 of the EHCR. However, in an extreme example of neglect, *Z v the United Kingdom* [2001] ECCR 233, the European Court of Human Rights found that a local authority had breached the fundamental Article 3 rights of four children not to be subjected to inhuman or degrading treatment. Social workers had knowledge of their 'appalling' living conditions over at least five years and reasonable steps should have been taken to remove them from that environment earlier. That judgement was considering practice in the 1980s, prior to the Children Act 1989 and the Human Rights Act 1998. Since that period, the law and guidance on child neglect has been substantially developed:

- Local authorities have powers and duties to provide services that will prevent neglect.

- Child protection inquiries are obligatory if a local authority has cause to suspect a child in their area is suffering significant harm from neglect.

- There are detailed child protection procedures to be followed carefully by all agencies involved.

- Where court intervention is being considered, the pre-proceedings process should be followed and parents made fully aware of the basis of the concerns.

- In a care order application, the court requires specific evidence linking the facts of the case to the assessment that an order is necessary.

- Local authorities continue with responsibilities to children who are or have been looked after who have been disadvantaged by neglect.

FURTHER READING AND RESOURCES

Legislation and guidance

All references to statute and regulations can be found at www.legislation.gov.uk.

Statutory guidance for England is published at www.gov.uk by the DfE.

Social Care Wales – The Learning Hub hosts copies of all the regulations, statutory guidance, and codes of practice that support Part 3 (assessment), Part 4 (planning), and Part 6 (looked after children) of the Social Services and Well-being (Wales) Act 2014: https://socialcare.wales/hub/sswbact

Policy and guidance in Northern Ireland – Department of Health: https://www.health-ni.gov.uk/topics/social-services, and Safeguarding Board Northern Ireland: https://www.proceduresonline.com/sbni/index.html#

Policy and guidance in Scotland – Scottish Government: https://www.gov.scot/about/how-government-is-run/directorates/children-and-families/

Case law

Court judgements are available at www.bailii.com and Find Case Law, https://caselaw.nationalarchives.gov.uk/

Other resources

NSPCC – case reviews: https://learning.nspcc.org.uk/case-reviews

NSPCC – systems in Northern Ireland and Scotland: https://learning.nspcc.org.uk/child-protection-system

National Adoption Service for Wales – Good Practice Guide on Adoption Support: https://www.adoptcymru.com/good-practice-guides

National Institute of Clinical Excellence (NICE) guidelines on recognising and responding to abuse and neglect in children: https://www.nice.org.uk/guidance/ng76

Research in Practice guidance on supporting parents in pre-proceedings – open access resources: https://bit.ly/3kgIU3X

Chapter 3
The impact of child neglect

INTRODUCTION

The impact of neglect on children's development is widely recognised. It is increasingly reported as having a more severe effect on a child's development than any other type of abuse (Howe, 2005), being harmful to a child's emotional, cognitive and behavioural development, physical development, and impacting severely on their overall sense of well-being (Stevenson, 2005). Of all the forms of child maltreatment, neglect is acknowledged as the most dangerous because of its potentially long-term and profoundly negative effects which have the potential to be permanent. These can impact a child's health, education, emotional and behavioural development, sense of identity, social and family relationships, and self-care skills. In the most serious cases, a child can die due to neglect (Beesley, 2011).

The impact of neglect on a child is dependent on the individual child and specific actions of the parent/s or carer/s. The impact can range from a temporary delay in a child's developmental progress, to significant and long-term consequences throughout an individual's life (Horwath, 2007). This chapter considers the impact of neglect on children with regards to severity, length and exposure to neglectful behaviour. It explores what we know about the effect of neglect on brain development. It also acknowledges the range of associated and compounding factors that can be commonly present within a household, parents' and carers' own experiences of neglectful parenting, and what protective factors could mitigate and ameliorate the impact of neglect on children and foster their resilience.

SEVERITY, LENGTH, EXPOSURE

Neglect can cause poor school attainment, delayed development and low self-esteem (NSPCC, 2015a and b), poor emotional and mental health, and can result in poor social skills and isolation (Action for Children, 2010; Sharley, 2018). In fact, the effects can continue throughout an individual's life and can affect the way in which relationships are formed, increase the likelihood of unemployment or holding unskilled roles, and ultimately inform how individuals parent their own children (Horwath, 2007). For these reasons, it is important that neglect is identified as early as possible and prevented through the provision of universal and early intervention services (Sharley, 2018). Failure to meet key developmental milestones throughout early childhood significantly amplifies the effect of neglect later in the child's adolescence (Schore, 2002). A child's early experiences impact on their brain development, in turn affecting their emotional, behavioural and cognitive development (Twardosz and Lutzker, 2010; Welsh Government, 2016a). Brain growth is heavily reliant on satisfactory nutrition, with malnourishment affecting the child's physical growth and bone development (Horwath, 2013). This means that poor diet and deficiencies will affect children's behaviour, their ability to learn, and their academic activity (Kerr *et al*, 2000; Polonko, 2006). Stress experienced by a child in utero due to domestic abuse, substance misuse or alcoholism may result in inadequate nutrition to the child (Monk *et al*, 2013). This can result in long-term consequences for a developing foetus, and may mean that the child is born smaller and/or prematurely, which can further be associated with a developmental propensity for physical, cognitive, social and behavioural difficulties (Hildyard and Wolfe, 2002; Talge *et al*, 2007; Sharley, 2018).

Children who may be exposed to chronic or persistent neglect over time may be likely to experience more severe and long-term effects of cumulative developmental problems (Truman, 2004). That is not to say that a "one-off" episode of neglect may be less severe, as this can also result in significant or permanent harm or even child fatality. A one-off episode of neglect (such as a child being burnt by a fire or hot saucepan due to lack of appropriate supervision) may be severe, and may be the reason for the child becoming known to statutory services. It can result in services becoming aware that a child has been living with persistent neglect over an extended period of time (Horwath, 2013; Sharley, 2018).

The impact of neglect on a child can differ depending on the type and severity of neglect, length of exposure, and their age and developmental stage. Neglect can produce both short- and long-term consequences for child development. Living in an emotionally abusive or neglectful environment, such as witnessing domestic abuse, being left unsupervised for long periods of time, or experiencing the insecurity of being left in the care of strangers, can leave children exposed to extended periods of stress (Doyle and Timms, 2014; Sharley, 2018). This could mean that an individual cannot regulate their emotions and/ or may have difficulty in managing interpersonal relationships later in life. The effects of neglect are variable and often described as being on a spectrum. There are two key factors to consider when assessing the impact of neglect – the length of time spent in the neglectful environment, and the child's age.

NEGLECT FROM AN ATTACHMENT PERSPECTIVE

Children develop strategies for ensuring that their needs are met. These attachment patterns develop from the child–caregiver interactions depending on the way in which the parent or caregiver may respond to the child's needs. When a parent or carer is available and consistent, responding in an effective and kind way, it is usual for a child to develop a secure attachment (Beesley, 2011). However, neglectful parenting can in some cases be the cause of formation of insecure attachment between a baby and a caregiver, when parents are anxious, annoyed or withdrawn and unable to provide a compassionate emotional response to the infant (Horwath, 2007). This type of attachment may be more likely to occur when parents or carers are emotionally unavailable to their child, for example, during incidents of mental-ill health, domestic abuse or substance misuse or addiction.

ATTACHMENT

Attachment is talked about widely in social work and social care. Attachment theory is helpful in understanding and assessing a child–parent/carer relationship and experiences that have taken place within early childhood. It can also help carers support children who have experienced trauma through neglect or inadequate care, to attune their own approach to parenting. Attachment relates to the close connections and trust a child has with those around them and is a universal phenomenon not related to ethnicity or culture (Cairns and Cairns, 2016). Attachment is a human desire to seek proximity to an adult or someone who is caring for them in order to protect them from danger. The attachment does not need to be to a mother, as studies from the 1960s suggested (Bowlby, 1969); it can be to any caregiver who spends a lot of time caring for and nurturing a child. Children develop proximity-promoting attachment behaviours; these include attracting the caregiver's attention by positively reaching out, smiling and cooing, or negatively by crying and protesting in an attempt to get the caregiver to soothe them. As children develop and can move around, they will follow, touch and cling to the caregiver. The baby's attachment behaviours should lead the caregiver to respond to them. The responsive and sensitive caregiver will react to a baby when they are hungry, lonely, cold or uncomfortable. The requests and responses are repeated constantly. The experience of requesting and having needs met creates what is known as a secure base (Schofield and Beek, 2014; 2018) (see also Chapter 8).

The secure base allows the child to feel settled and content so that they can be confident to explore their environment. When this responsive caregiving can be relied on, this optimises social and physical development. When a child has not experienced attuned or responsive care that promotes security, as in the case of child neglect, children will experience fear and uncertainty. Where children find that their carer is unpredictable and they cannot rely on their reactions, or trust has been broken, then a child may feel unsupported, alone and begin to have difficulty trusting other people in their lives. This can lead to what is known as attachment difficulties.

Attachment patterns develop in response to different types of caregiving. Early studies by Ainsworth and Bell (1970) found two different attachment patterns that developed in relation to poor and neglectful parenting: insecure-avoidant and insecure-ambivalent/resistant (Schofield and Beek, 2014). Some of the behaviours of young people who have experienced abuse and neglect might include being less able to discriminate in their approaches to other children and adults (Schofield and Beek, 2018) and appearing to show more affection for unfamiliar adults. This arises from carers who may be inconsistent in their caregiving to a child – at times they may be very responsive and then later they do not meet the child's needs.

Caregivers may lack understanding of the child's needs, or may sometimes place their own needs before the child's. The challenge for the child in this environment is that they are struggling to understand the unpredictability of whether or not their needs will be met sufficiently. As the child is not able to learn how to predict the response they will receive, they may increase strategies such as crying, whining, or being more anxious in an attempt to get a response. When the child gets the response they hope for, they are ambivalent and may be difficult to soothe. Horwath (2007) identifies that neglectful caregiving can lead to a third attachment strategy, disorganised attachment. Children who have formed a disorganised style of attachment have done so because they have been unable to find a safe way of obtaining interest and attention from their caregiver/s.

Brain development in the early years

Whilst our brains develop throughout our lives, beginning from before birth, there are key periods during early childhood and then adolescence when brains are more sensitive and more affected by experiences – both positively and negatively (NSPCC, 2021b). According to De Bellis (2005) elevated levels of chemicals in the brain related to stress reactions result in adverse brain development in children in early life. Those children who experience insecurity or confusion through neglectful caregiving may develop altered regions of the brain that facilitate the ability to process language and speech (Howe, 2000). Neglect can impede the development of the prefrontal cortical regions (De Bellis, 2005), increasing the likelihood of learning disability, inattention and poor academic achievement. It can also lead to passivity and a child's incapacity to process, or tolerate, strong negative and positive experiences (Doyle and Timms, 2014). If neuronal pathways are not stimulated adequately, they are likely to "wither" (Horwath, 2007), meaning a lower likelihood of reaching their full developmental potential (Durkan et al, 2015; Welsh Government, 2016a). This means that children who have experienced prolonged or frequent neglectful caregiving may be more likely to have difficulty articulating emotions. They may become confused when differentiating between feelings shown by others, and may not know how to respond to them effectively (Pollack et al, 2000).

The NSPCC's 'Sharing the Brain Story' summarises child development using six metaphors developed in the US (by FrameWorks Institute and Centre on the Developing Child at Harvard University). They have since been tested and adapted for use in the UK (NSPCC, 2021b) to provide understanding on child development with a focus on how family life can be improved and how neglect and abuse can be prevented. There is a useful short YouTube animated clip that explains the metaphors (see the list of websites at the end of this chapter). The six metaphors presented in the booklet are set out below.

1. Brain architecture	Brains are built through a process that begins before birth and is ongoing into adulthood. The building process happens in a sequence which begins with laying the foundations, shaping the rooms, then later wiring the electrical systems. These need to happen in the correct order. A child's early experiences shape how the brain is built. A strong foundation increases the chances of positive health and learning later on, whilst a weak foundation increases the odds of difficulties. Having negative experiences early on does not always set a child on a fixed path, but can result in mental health problems, drug abuse or diabetes and cardiovascular disease.
2. Serve and return	Like the "serve and return" interactions in a good game of tennis, children reach out for interaction with adults through gestures and imitating facial expressions. This helps them develop language, cognitive and social skills that actively build a child's brain. If a caregiver does not respond and return these noises and gestures, the interaction will break down, interrupting the child's developmental process, resulting in negative implications for later learning.

3. The stress metaphor	Harmful or toxic stress happens when a child experiences severe or persistent stress such as the impact of poverty, neglect or violence – without consistent supportive relationships. Harmful stress is brought on by prolonged exposure to traumatic situations or experiences such as neglectful care. It will impact the way in which a child's brain develops and can lead to lifelong problems with learning, behaviour and health.
4. Air traffic control	Children's ability to remember, focus and pay attention is like the air traffic control system at a busy airport. Planes need to fly and land at the same time as others need to take off! But there is only so much room on the ground and in the air. Children need to manage their airspace, to complete tasks, manage activities and relationships.
5. Overloaded	If a lorry carries too much weight, it can be overloaded to the point of breaking down. When parents are burdened with stresses like poverty or lack of support, the weight of these problems can also overload their mental and emotional capacity to take care of their children's emotional needs. Support can be provided to overloaded parents that offloads sources of stress, helping them to improve their capacity to care.
6. Tipping the scales	If you think of child development as a scale – we want the scale to tip towards the positive side. Positive things like supportive relationships, "serve and returns", and calm and nurturing are all beneficial for this. Negative things like toxic stress, i.e. neglectful parenting, tip towards the other side. If we can load the positive side with as much weight as possible (in the form of support to develop coping skills), it will make it more difficult to tip the scales to negative. This is called resilience.

(NSPCC, 2021b)

Brain development during adolescence

Brain development is also crucial during adolescence, which affects the pre-frontal cortex. This is responsible for impulse control and is crucial for decision-making (Beesley, 2011). During adolescence, young people are more likely to be impulsive and undertake risk-taking behaviour, and need the guidance of a parent, carer or trusted adult. Young people who have grown up living with neglect are considered more vulnerable to these behaviours, with little access to appropriate support. Behaviours can include but are not limited to self-harm, anti-social behaviour, child exploitation, drug and alcohol misuse, being described by their caregivers or school as being "beyond control", going missing, or running away (Beesley, 2011). In fact, in 2019 neglect was the most common form of harm for adolescents who were on the child protection register or subject to a child protection plan in England and Northern Ireland (and the second most common in Wales and Scotland) (NSPCC, 2020). This may be surprising, as it is easy to assume that as children become older and desire more independence, they may need less care and support than those who are younger. However, whilst the form of care may change with age, it is crucial that young people have stable relationships and access to support and guidance during their transition into adulthood. This is more of a challenge for social work practice as it is often at a time when young people will also no longer have regular contact with teachers or professionals in schools or colleges (NSPCC, 2020).

The signs of neglect are often harder to spot in older children, as they may have devised strategies to cover it up, to hide it from other young people and the adults around them. Young people themselves may not be aware they are being neglected. Additionally, the risks neglect poses may be different:

> *The signs of neglect of older children may be more difficult to identify than signs of neglect in younger children, and older children may present with different risks. For example, older children may want to spend more time away from a neglectful home, and, given their experience of neglect, they may be more vulnerable to risks such as going missing, offending behaviour or exploitation.*

> (Care Quality Commission, 2018, p.1)

Spending time away from home, a common feature of neglected children, creates risk for young people who may be the targets of sexual and criminal exploitation, radicalisation, or of gang-related activity or violence (see Chapter 7).

Some of the difficulties of working with older children are that parents and professionals assume that young people are less vulnerable and have more agency. Parents and professionals can also view the presenting behavioural issues by the child as the problem, and do not always think of what lies behind the behaviour. When a child's behaviour becomes the sole problem, those around them do not always consider the context of the impact of neglect.

Neglect can lead to problems in adolescence and adulthood including, but not limited to:

- poor mental and physical health;

- difficulties with interpersonal relationships;

- offending behaviour;

- substance misuse;

- a high propensity for risk-taking behaviour;

- suicide.

(Care Quality Commission, 2018)

A review of services for neglected young people was undertaken by four inspectorates in 2018. Their report, entitled *Growing up Neglected: A Multi-agency Response to Older Children*, found that there are very few services or interventions for this group and many of the resources available to professionals are designed to assess and respond to neglect in younger children. Older children, however, may have been neglected throughout their childhood and can carry this profound legacy into adolescence. This sometimes means that young people are not well equipped to cope with the many trials and tribulations that adolescence brings and may be poorly supported to manage this transition. Here we can see the importance of chronologies (also referred to in Chapter 4 in the assessment of neglect) being kept and updated by professionals, so workers can consider the history and impact of previous and ongoing neglect. Even when neglect has stopped and children have been living in improved and stable situations in foster care or adoption for quite some time, the trauma from earlier childhood may recur in later childhood and adolescence (see Chapter 6).

THE IMPACT OF NEGLECT ON DEVELOPMENTAL NEEDS

Beesley (2011, p. 57) sets out the impact of neglect on children across seven areas.

Health	Failure to thrive, developmental delay, dental caries, illnesses and infections, lack of immunisation, substance misuse, unsafe sexual activity

Education	Poor play skills, delayed speech and language development, low academic achievement, poor cognitive skills, poor school attendance, misconduct at school, compromised employment opportunities
Emotional and behavioural development	Anxious or disordered attachments, lack of empathy, inability to manage stress, inability to control impulses, conduct disorder, withdrawn, aggressive
Identity	Poor self-image and self-esteem, lack of sense of belonging, negative impact on ethnic and cultural identify
Family and social relationships	Poor peer relationships, isolated, subject to bullying and rejection by peers, lack of appropriate adult role models
Social presentation	Dirty, smelly, lack of appropriate clothing impacting on social relationships and sense of belonging, lack of involvement in community
Self-care skills	Lack of problem-solving skills, overly dependent, self-reliant and inappropriately independent, lack of confidence and competence.

ASSOCIATED AND COMPOUNDING FACTORS

Children who experience abuse or neglect, stressful or poor-quality childhoods, and who are brought up in households where there is domestic abuse, alcohol or drug misuse may be more likely to adopt health-harming and anti-social behaviours in adult life (Bellis *et al*, 2016). Adverse Childhood Experiences (ACEs) are traumatic events that occur in childhood, such as being a victim of neglect or abuse, being exposed to parental alcohol or substance misuse, incidents of domestic abuse, or criminal incarceration. Children who have ACEs are more likely to have unsolved interpersonal problems regarding trust and dependency in later life. Bellis *et al* (2016) argue that individuals who experience ACEs in childhood often end up trying to raise their own children in households where adversities are more common. This can mean that childhood understandings of relationships might also inform a person's approach towards their own parenting, potentially creating a generational cycle of adversity. This could impinge on a parent's ability to notice the child's cues, or even understand that a response is required by the child (Crittenden, 1992). Neglectful parenting can occur when the parent or carer is not fully attuned to the child or young person's needs and does not understanding which actions are likely to cause which outcomes in the child's behaviours (Horwath, 2007). ACEs are discussed in more detail in Chapter 6. Attunement is further discussed in Chapter 8 in relation to interventions and Video-Interactive Guidance.

WORKING WITH CHILDREN WITH COMPLEX NEEDS/CHILDREN WITH DISABILITIES

Literature on neglect is divided as to whether children with additional needs are more vulnerable to child neglect, or whether families' inevitable engagement with a range of professionals may make them more visible to inspection (Horwath, 2013). It is acknowledged that children with disabilities can be more likely to experience multiple forms and multiple incidences of maltreatment and can be perceived as more susceptible to neglect due to their separation from other children, and the lack of control they may have over their own bodies and lives (Sobsey and Doe, 1991; Sullivan and Knutson, 2000). Taylor et al's (2014) study into children with disabilities and child protection in Scotland found that children with disabilities were more likely to experience maltreatment than children without disabilities, and likely to experience more than one form of maltreatment. That said, children with disabilities may be increasingly predisposed to neglect due to the increased caring duties, medical needs or complex routines that their disability demands from their parent or caregiver (DePanfilis, 2006).

Beesley (2011) suggests that it can be helpful to consider the parent–child relationship to reflect on how the parent views their caring role. If the main focus of the parenting is on meeting the disabled child's basic physical or medical needs, then it could be that the child's emotional needs may be neglected. It is important to remember that while caring for a child with disabilities can bring added strain for a parent/carer, it should not forgive inadequate levels of parenting or neglect. Doing the best one can as a parent/carer for a child is not the same as good enough parenting (Horwath, 2002). Kennedy and Wonnacott (2005) offer a model towards understanding, suggesting the neglect of children with disabilities to be a result of the interaction between *disabling barriers* and the *capacity of the child's parents to parent*.

REFLECTIVE EXERCISE

● Would this situation be acceptable for a child without disabilities?

● Are the child's emotional and psychological needs being met? Or is there an increased focus on their physical development and medical needs and/or care?

- Does the presence of care and love hide the parent or carer's inability to meet the child's needs sufficiently?

- Is there a difference between neglect due to poverty and neglect due to lack of emotional resources? Parents or carers caring for a child with disabilities may be struggling financially; the lack of provision of care may be connected to this.

- Has the child received all of their dental and immunisation appointments?

(Messages for practice adapted from Kennedy and Wonnacott, 2005, p. 248)

PARENTS' AND CARERS' EXPERIENCES

Although it is not always possible to determine the causes of neglect, there are some key features or forerunners that appear to be connected. For example, parents or carers may have poorer parenting and problem-solving skills. The term "toxic trio" is widely used to describe the co-occurrence of mental health problems, substance misuse and domestic abuse within a family (CAADA, 2014). In their study into practitioner perceptions of child neglect in England, Horwath and Bishop (2001) found that domestic abuse was an issue in over one-fifth of all neglect cases. The study identified that alcohol misuse (31%), domestic abuse (22%) and mental health issues (14%) were the three most common types of parenting issues present in cases of child neglect. Whilst parents' and caregivers' needs are important, it can be possible for practitioners to lose focus on the child's lived experience of neglectful parenting. Although it is important to work in partnership with children and young people's parents and carers, adults' needs should not detract from the primary focus of protecting and safeguarding a child from the harm caused by neglect (Rees *et al*, 2021a). When a practitioner is focusing on parents' difficulties, it is always important to check and revisit support plans to monitor whether any changes made have had a positive impact on the child/ren. This point is highlighted in the *Working Together to Safeguard Children* national policy guidance, which emphasises the importance of maintaining a focus on children's needs, rather than focusing on the needs of adults.

A desire to think the best of adults and to hope they can overcome their difficulties should not subvert the need to protect children from chaotic, abusive and neglectful homes. Social workers and practice supervisors should always reflect the latest research on the impact of abuse and

*neglect and relevant findings from serious case and practice reviews
when analysing the level of need and risk faced by the child. This should
be reflected in the case recording.*

(HM Government, 2019, p. 31)

CASE STUDY: LUCY

You are working with Lucy and her family. Lucy is five years old and
has additional learning needs. She is one of five children. Both of
Lucy's parents work full time. A referral has been made to children's
services from the health practitioner that states that in the time they
have been working with Lucy, 13 of her appointments have been
cancelled and four rearranged. Originally, when they had begun
working with Lucy, Lucy's mother was not working and was able
to take Lucy to all the appointments. The family are not previously
known to children's services. The referral says that Lucy has global
developmental delay, she is a non-verbal child who struggles to
play and make friends. Lucy attends a mainstream primary school.
Previously, Lucy's parents have minimised her additional needs
and struggle to acknowledge her uniqueness – they have previously
declined two voluntary health assessments.

From reading the referral, you believe that Lucy is being neglected
and her basic needs are not being met by her parents. You feel that
her parents are dismissive of her needs and have disengaged from
the health practitioner's care planning. The referral says that the
health practitioner has been unable to assess Lucy's neurological
and developmental wellbeing and is concerned that she is at risk of
significant harm. You decide that an urgent strategy discussion is
needed to assess whether Lucy is at risk of or is currently living with
neglect.

You approach your manager to request a strategy discussion.
Your manager advises you that he does not believe Lucy is at any
immediate risk of harm and that a voluntary assessment can be
undertaken in these circumstances. Further, if Lucy's parents do
not keep the assessment appointment then your manager says to
close the case. Whilst you accept this initial decision, you continue
to have concerns. You are aware that Lucy's parents struggle to
trust professionals due to their own poor childhood experiences
of statutory intervention. However, you have made an appointment
to see Lucy at home to undertake a child in need assessment.
Unfortunately, 30 minutes before the appointment, Lucy's mother
texts you to inform you that she has 'forgotten the appt and can we
rearrange?'.

You return to your manager, who remains of the position that the threshold has not been met for a child protection enquiry, but that a voluntary assessment remains appropriate and is offered to the family.

You are questioning what it takes for the threshold for "significant harm" to be met in cases of neglect as you are worried about the impact on Lucy.

What would you do now? How would you evidence the impact of neglect on Lucy?

Questions:

- What is the severity, length and exposure to neglect?

- What is Lucy's age and developmental stage?

- Are Lucy's needs being met? If not, why not?

- How do Lucy's parents' experiences of being parented impact on their caregiving?

- What factors may mitigate Lucy's experiences of neglect?

- How can you capture the impact of neglectful parenting?

(Joel Price, Independent Reviewing Officer/social worker)

Mitigation and amelioration

This chapter has explored the impact of neglect on children. Neglect can cause delay to a child's developmental process or result in significant and long-term health problems that impact an individual's life (Horwath, 2017). That said, not all children who have experienced neglect will respond in the same way. In fact, identical actions by a parent or carer can affect individual children or young people within the same household in a very different way (Daniel *et al*, 2011). There are a number of protective factors that (as mentioned earlier in the chapter) can help to "tip the scales" towards the positive side for children, and foster their resilience (NSPCC, 2021b). Resilience is discussed in more detail in Chapter 8.

FURTHER READING AND RESOURCES

Websites

NSPCC (2021) *Impact of Neglect*, available at: https://bit.ly/3GBDCHv

NSPCC (2021) *How do Childhood Experiences Affect Brain Development?*, available at: https://bit.ly/3QAuebV

Video

NSPCC (2017) *How a Child's Brain Develops Through Early Experiences.* Brain Builders Video, YouTube, available at: https://bit.ly/3QEt7rr

Practice and policy briefings

Baynes P (2020) *Life Story Work: Why does it matter?*, available at: https://bit.ly/3iD25nO

Chapter 4
Recognising and assessing child neglect

INTRODUCTION

Identifying neglect is not a straightforward task in practice. As we discussed in Chapter 1, child neglect is not only the most prevalent form of maltreatment in the UK; it is also widely recognised as being the most complex. Dependent on your personal and professional background, and the organisational context in which you are based, what you consider neglect to be (and the potential support you offer), will vary considerably. This chapter explores the practice challenges of recognising and assessing neglect and the impact of these factors on its early identification. In particular, it considers the difficulty of assessing and responding to child neglect in the growing context of poverty and austerity in the UK. The chapter visits themes including professional judgement and decision making, talking and listening to children, organisational factors, poverty, the diversion of parental needs, feminising neglect, and knowing when "enough is enough" in the context of thresholds for interventiion.

DECISION-MAKING AND ASSESSMENT TOOLS

Assessing whether a child is living with neglect is not an easy process. Neglect is multi-faceted in nature, often having more than one cause, and rarely based on one specific incident (Holland *et al*, 2013; NSPCC, 2015a and b). It also centres on an act of omission, a parent or carer's failure to meet a child's needs, as opposed to an act of commission, such as physical abuse. Assessing the absence of something rather than evidencing the presence of physical or sexual abuse can make the task more challenging and it can be a struggle to identify and judge when parenting is considered neglectful, and a threshold for intervention has been reached (Wilkinson and Bower, 2017). Although there are many assessment tools and frameworks to help practitioners make more evidence-based and objective decisions about whether a child is being neglected, this does not necessarily mean that they always provide practitioners with the "right" answers. There can also be challenges for practitioners in understanding their intuitive or visceral experiences when walking into a neglectful home environment, whether the home is dirty, has a strong smell of detritus, or is extremely clean (Ferguson, 2016).

Horwath (no date) developed a tool for Calderdale Safeguarding Children Partnership and Safeguarding Adults Board that can help make sense of an individual's lived experiences to assist practitioners in assessing and intervening in cases of neglect (this is provided under the list of further resources at the end of this chapter).

The Framework for Assessment of Children in Need and their Families

In statutory practice in England and Wales, the assessment of children and their families is commonly undertaken using *The Framework for Assessment of Children in Need and their Families* (DH, 2000). The assessment framework takes an ecological approach using a triangle: child's developmental needs, parenting capacity, and family and environmental factors. Principles underpinning the assessment framework include:

- Child-centred

- Being rooted in child development

- Are ecological in their approach

- Ensure quality of opportunity

- Involve working with children and families

- Build on strengths as well as identify difficulties

- Are inter-agency in their approach to assessment and the provision of services

- Are a continuing process, not a single event

- Are carried out in parallel with other action and providing services

- Are grounded in evidence-based knowledge

(DH, 2000, p.10)

Home Conditions Assessment Tool

The Home Conditions Assessment Tool was recommended by the Department of Health in the *Framework for Assessment of Children in Need and their Families* document (2000), and is based on Davie *et al's*

(1984) Family Cleanliness Scale. The tool provides practitioners with a mental checklist of 11 items to be observed during home visits. As with any assessment method, it should not be used in isolation, but it can offer a framework to monitor a parent or carer's progress or deterioration in terms of the conditions in the household over a period of time. Whilst the tool can be helpful as a basic guide for social workers to assess the physical aspects of a child's home environment, it has been criticised for its inability to engage with the more pervasive issues of neglect. Since its production, there have been a number of variations of the tool adapted by specific UK local authorities, which are widely available online.

Graded Care Profile 2 Assessment Tool

Tools such as the Graded Care Profile 2 (GCP2) have been used widely in England and Wales specifically to assess concerns of neglect. The GCP2 is an updated version of the Graded Care Profile, developed in 1995 to measure quality of care across four domains (based on Maslow's Hierarchy of Needs): physical, safety, love and esteem. It has been found to be reliable and effective (Johnson et al, cited by Smith et al, 2019). The tool supports practitioners to grade the level of care given to a child across four areas: physical care, care of safety, emotional care and developmental care. The tool and associated training for the GCP2 can improve practitioners' understandings of, and confidence in, their ability to evidence neglect, and communication of concerns to other agencies (Smith et al, 2019). The GCP2 can be completed by engaging the wider professional network to evidence positive change across services, for example, by statutory services and a school nurse or health visitor. (Working with other agencies in a multi-agency context is explored in more detail in Chapter 5.) That said, criticisms of the GCP2's assessment framework include its length and its inability to address specific areas such as adolescent neglect (explored in more detail in Chapters 1 and 5).

Limitations of frameworks and tools

Whilst it can be beneficial to be guided by a specific assessment model or tool to help identify different aspects of levels of neglect, the use of scales and tools when assessing a child's experiences of neglect also have their limitations (Horwath, 2007). The few assessment tools mentioned here all have their shortcomings and are largely based on the practitioner's own beliefs about what they consider adequate care, that is, their professional judgement and the personal biases this may include – as explored in Chapter 1.

THE IMPORTANCE OF PROFESSIONAL JUDGEMENT

Professional judgement is an important aspect of any assessment process. However, it is central when assessing whether or not a child has been, or is being, subjected to neglectful parenting. This is because, aside from the different types of neglect that may be present, practitioners still need to make a social and professional judgement about the standard of care that is being provided to the child by their caregiver, and essentially whether their needs have been met sufficiently (Horwath, 2013). Families, friendship groups or communities often do not hold the same ideas on raising children, nor the same values and beliefs around what constitutes an acceptable or unacceptable standard of care. Norms around the care of children are commonly affected by cultural views and social factors. What is considered appropriate by one individual, within one culture or group, at a specific point in time will not be considered appropriate by another individual within the same group or at the same point in time. For example, this can be seen in cultural attitudes towards physical chastisement and the smacking of children in UK nations. The smacking of children was banned in Scotland in 2020 and Wales in 2022, whilst remaining legal along with other forms of punishment (in certain circumstances) in England and Northern Ireland under the "reasonable chastisement" defence (Children Act, 2004). These attitudes and norms bring challenges even before the further question of intentionality is raised. Professional role is also central in influencing judgements about whether or not a child is living with neglect, and these can be informed or embedded within organisational structures, categories, and the interpretation of legal thresholds and definitions (Beesley, 2011). The use of photographs of neglectful environments can offer visual support for reflective discussions, and can help practitioners avoid misinterpretation or subjective interpretation of words.

TALKING AND LISTENING TO CHILDREN

In all aspects of their lives, children have the right to be heard and their views and wishes considered in decisions about their lives. When identifying and assessing neglect, it is important to really understand a child's lived experience of neglect and the impact it has or is having on them. What is it like living in a dirty or neglected home? Are they cold, hungry, are they alone, do they need a bath or their nappy changing? Who is helping them get ready for school? Is there any food in the cupboards (Beesley, 2011)? To do this, it is crucial to see the child in their home environment and to observe interactions between them and their carers or family members. Practitioners should also make time to explain to a child what is happening when they visit, create space to listen to children and hear their views and experiences, and also to communicate with the purpose of understanding their experiences (Talking and Listening to Children Project (TLC), 2022).

Both UK legislation and the United Nations Convention on the Rights of the Child (1990) (Article 12 – respect for the views of the child) place the child's welfare as paramount when making decisions about their lives. The policy guidance *Working Together to Safeguard Children* (DfE) specifically states that 'every assessment should reflect the unique characteristics of the child within their family and community context. Each child whose referral has been accepted by children's social care should have their individual needs assessed, including analysis of the parental capacity to meet those needs' (p. 30) and that 'every assessment must be informed by the views of the child as well as the family, and a child's wishes and feelings must be sought regarding the provision of services to be delivered' (p. 22).

The Talking and Listening to Children Project (TLC, 2022) is a four-nation UK research project that was funded by the Economic and Social Research Council (ESRC) to explore how social workers communicate with children in their everyday practice. The TLC project has a comprehensive website which offers useful videos about communication, and signposting to a wider range of alternative resources, including books and papers on communicating effectively with children. The project introduces the Child-Case-Context model, an ecological model for communication to understand encounters or meetings that take place between a child or young person and their worker (see: www.talkingandlisteningtochildren.co.uk).

PRACTITIONER TIPS

- Children and young people have a right to be listened to and their wishes and feelings taken into account in planning and decision-making about them.

- The child's voice can easily get lost in cases of neglect – be aware of the potential barriers to hearing the child.

- Neglected children are at risk of being unseen and unheard – they may present as passive and self-contained, or touch-hungry.

- Always keep the child at the centre of your thinking.

- Familiarise yourself with knowledge and skills for direct work with children and young people for your home visits.

- Ensure you have a range of resources in your "backpack" to carry out direct work.

- Utilise good supervision, support and training in working and communicating with children.

(Adapted from Beesley, 2011, p. 53)

THE IMPACT OF ORGANISATIONAL FACTORS

Organisational or professional factors impact significantly on what constitutes an acceptable level of parenting and care. Recognising and assessing neglect requires effective inter-agency work across different professional groups and organisations. Sharing observations and information is essential to safeguarding and protecting children living with neglect. Despite this, successful collaboration continues to be one of the largest and most persistent challenges to practice in neglect (Pithouse and Crowley, 2016). Barriers can include inadequate training in neglect identification, differing professional perspectives and understandings, lack of professional confidence in responding to neglect, divergent agency roles and organisational remits – to name a few (Sharley, 2019). These collaborative challenges are visited in more detail in Chapter 6 where the fundamental role of working with schools is discussed in greater depth.

The conceptual complexity of neglect discussed in Chapter 1 also raises obstacles in relation to how specific services respond to the issue, both in the referral of concerns and the involvement of assessments, with individual practitioners understanding, identifying and assessing concerns differently. This can arise across different services but also within the same social work team or organisation, which is exemplified in the following quote from a head teacher in Wales when talking about responding to neglect:

> What I find [is] different social workers, depending on who picked it up, there were different levels of concern and support within that. You work with one family and you'd have any support that they needed straight away. Whereas some others [social workers] were dismissive [of neglect] – so it wasn't like a level playing field: there wasn't sort of consistency from social worker to social worker.

(Head teacher)

In practice, it is important to acknowledge the difference between the broad understanding of child neglect (i.e. when a child is not having their needs met) and the much smaller operational category of neglect within statutory services (Daniel et al, 2011). Operational categories are commonly used to rationalise interventions and unlock access to scarce resources and support. Statutory thresholds are the categories that establish the minimum level of adequate care for a child and are reflective of whether a child is deemed in need of services or protection. In cases of neglect, operational categories identify what is deemed "neglectful" by the specific organisation and what intervention services at what level would be appropriate. This differentiation between the two definitions can make judging whether the care a child is receiving is "good enough" challenging, particularly in a multi-agency setting. When the further lens of personal and professional values and beliefs is added, and one's own experiences of being parented, this can make the task of judging whether a child is experiencing neglect (and to what extent) quite problematic (Truman, 2004). In addition to this, practitioners' approaches to noticing the presence of neglect and making referrals to statutory services can be further influenced by the views of colleagues and the opinions of service managers. Personal experience, feelings (or "intuition") and the referrer's expectations of the outcome of completing a statutory referral can all affect the decision to refer or not to refer (Horwath, 2007). With this in mind, Horwath (2007) suggests the addition of a "fourth domain" to the aforementioned assessment framework (of child's developmental needs; parenting capacity; and family and environmental factors), emphasising the notion of professional judgement, to include a "Practitioner's Domain" to analyse professional role, perception of services, personal feelings, community and perception of the team and manager.

Effective chronologies and case file recording

There are factors that can support the identification of neglect, including keeping clear and accurate case file recording and maintaining up-to-date chronologies. These are simple yet effective tools that, when used within inter-professional practice or in a multi-agency context, can assist children's practitioners with an overview of a child's experiences over a period of time and can help avoid cases drifting and interventions being delayed. Chronologies can help social workers to keep a record of events, observations or concerns that can help build a bigger picture and monitor a family's circumstances with the purpose of identifying patterns of inadequate care (or evidencing positive changes and improvements over time). These tools are useful methods for gathering and collating important information that can be used to inform the ongoing assessment of a child's needs (Horwath, 2013), providing an overview about frequency and severity of neglect, guiding the timely intervention of services and the provision of appropriate support and help. Practitioners in statutory services often compile multi-agency chronologies as a way of gathering and organising large amounts of information (HM Government, 2018), observations and knowledge about a family as part of their everyday case work. However, Rees *et al*

(2021a and b), when analysing child practice reviews, found that very few chronologies were being used in practice in Wales.

Key points for good recording practice:

- Including telephone and face-to-face contacts;

- Is current, up to date;

- Includes a chronology or genogram;

- Is concise and factual;

- Includes observation;

- Records parental attitudes;

- Records failures to attend appointments;

- Records evidence of non-compliance;

- Includes a plan of action;

- Includes the child's voice.

(Beesley, 2011, p.128)

Start Again Syndrome

Whilst chronologies are an effective way to gather and organise large amounts of information over an extended period of time, they can at times present an overwhelming picture of a household's circumstances. "Start Again Syndrome" refers to a practitioner or agency's decision to set aside the history of the case, and to "start again" afresh by only focusing on the present concerns (Brandon *et al*, 2008) rather than giving essential consideration to the history of the parents/carers and the patterns of risk within the case (Ferguson, 2016). There is potential for this to happen frequently – when there is a change in social worker, a case transferred to a colleague (NSPCC, 2022b) or team, or closed, a restructure, or the onward referral to a new agency. The major concern with taking a "start again" approach is that critical information and knowledge about the child's lived experience is lost. Whilst the child's story may be new to each worker, the ongoing experience of living with the harm caused by neglectful parenting persists for the child and continues to cumulatively impact on their health and development with each day that passes. Findings from children's case reviews undertaken in 2021 and 2022 where neglect was identified as a key factor highlighted that professionals *still* do not always recognise the signs of neglect, treating issues in isolation without addressing the causes or understanding the cumulative and long-term impact of neglect over time (NSPCC, 2022b).

NEGLECT AND POVERTY

Neglect is the form of maltreatment considered to be most closely linked with low socio-economic status (Spencer and Baldwin, 2005). In fact, children living in poverty in the UK are over-represented in the child protection system (Horwath, 2013), with families who live in poverty being 40 times more likely to be referred to social services (Bywaters et al, 2016). Living without money and access to basic resources brings added stress and anxiety for parents and carers and can undoubtedly impact on the ability to meet children's needs (Beesley, 2011). Conversely, financial hardship can also be the reason that families become known to services in the first place. Living in poverty does not predetermine the presence of neglect (Farmer and Lutman, 2012), but is acknowledged as a risk factor for children from lower socio-economic neighbourhoods being more likely to experience physical neglect than those from higher socio-economic communities (Shanahan et al, 2017). Whilst there is a strong association between neglect and lower socio-economic class, it is important to differentiate neglect from circumstances of poverty (Bywaters et al, 2016), as parents or carers experiencing financial hardship may not have access to the necessary resources the family requires.

Poverty can have a profound and long-term effect on children and their lives. However, despite its interconnected nature, practitioners can experience "poverty blindness" in practice through ambivalence, a lack of awareness or reluctance to get involved (Jack and Gill, 2003) or to stigmatise families who are living with poverty (Featherstone et al, 2018; Morris et al, 2018). This is explored in greater detail in Chapter 8.

Poverty-aware practice

Because of the relationship between poverty, inequality and neglect, it is important to consider the implications for families within safeguarding and child protection practice (Featherstone et al, 2019). In 2019, the British Association of Social Workers (BASW) produced an Anti-Poverty Practice Guide in collaboration with the Child Welfare Inequalities Project (CWIP). The guide was developed based on focus group consultations with BASW members across the UK. The guide supports practitioners who work with people living in poverty, offering practical skills-based approaches.

The box overleaf provides a summary of some of the approaches and skills outlined in the guide (BASW, 2019, p. 18) that engender anti-poverty practice. These points are particularly relevant in supporting practitioners who are working with families where child neglect may be a concern, and can help build an awareness of the local context of poverty, and unpick its impact on a family's circumstances and capabilities.

- **Understand local data:** develop a working knowledge of the geographical context. This is crucial to understanding local deprivation, ethnicity and population density.

- **Know your local community:** build an awareness of the organisational context you work in, the third sector providers, the religious organisations, and get to know and form relationships with the people at these services.

- **Build and maintain inter-agency alliances:** draw on your professional leadership skills and build alliances with individuals and organisations that can assist people experiencing poverty.

- **Involve families and communities:** develop routine practices that enable families and communities to provide you with feedback about the role of social work services in addressing poverty, so as to open up fresh approaches to community participation.

- **Relationship-based practice:** build trusting relationships with people in the context of shame and trauma and enable reflection on people's needs and experiences. Anchoring practice in values recognises that poverty violates people's rights to justice and socio-economic well-being.

- **Advocacy:** support practitioners to become confident in talking about poverty, income and their consequences (with knowledge of welfare benefits and support services).

- **Supervision:** supervisors need supporting to understand the relationship between poverty and harm, the impact of poverty, and the role of social workers in addressing socioeconomic hardship.

(BASW, 2019, p. 18)

At the heart of poverty-aware practice is understanding the context in which you are working. The guide suggests that recognising yourself as part of the community in which you work can help you "co-locate" yourself in the challenges experienced by the families that you are supporting. Taking a relationship-based approach to practice will offer a route to understand people's life experiences and histories through providing them with space to tell their stories and understand the determinants of harm (BASW, 2019).

AVOIDING FOCUS ON PARENTAL NEEDS

The challenges and problems that parents and carers face can impact on their ability to provide adequate care and result in the neglect of their children (Horwath, 2013). Parents may have poorer parenting skills compared to other non-neglectful parents or carers (Brayden et al, 1992). For parents or caregivers who neglect their children, there appears to be an increased lack of capacity to deal with children's behaviour in terms of co-operation and boundary setting. A lower parental educational level is also associated with a greater risk of neglect occurring (Scannapieco and Connell-Carrick, 2005), with further vulnerability for children who are cared for by parents with a learning disability, history of maltreatment themselves, who have attempted suicide, or who have mental health or substance misuse problems (McKeganey et al, 2002; Carter and Myers, 2007). We explore the impact of Adverse Childhood Experiences in more detail in Chapter 5.

A key message, however, recurrent in findings from child safeguarding practice reviews in England and child practice reviews in Wales is that in neglect cases there is too often a focus on adults' problems, to the detriment of the child's needs (Brandon et al, 2020), with children's voices rarely being heard (see also Chapters 2 and 8). Practice reviews are undertaken on a small number of cases when a child dies or is seriously harmed or injured as a consequence of abuse or neglect. Neglect is a factor in most reviews undertaken. In England, neglect was found to be present in three-quarters of child practice reviews analysed in 2020 (Brandon et al, 2020). Whilst neglect is only the primary cause of death or harm in 19 per cent of cases, it is acknowledged as being present in most children's lives alongside other types of maltreatment (when a child dies and when a child is seriously injured) (Brandon et al, 2020, p. 54).

FEMINISING NEGLECT

When identifying and assessing neglect in practice, there has tended to be a focus on mothers as opposed to fathers (Moran, 2009). Research has suggested that neglect practice is highly gendered with a particular focus on women (Daniel and Taylor, 2006). This may reflect the assumption that women continue to be the primary caregivers in our society (Horwath, 2013), that most families receiving support from statutory child protection services are lone mothers (Daniel and Taylor, 2006), and/or that the act of caring is traditionally presented and statistically represented as women's work (Turney, 2000). However, practitioners must be mindful of gender issues in practice specifically where mothers or women are exclusively implicated in issues of inadequate parenting or care of their children (Turney, 2000), as policies in child protection, and specifically in neglect practice, do not commonly and clearly address issues of gender (Daniel and Taylor, 2006).

In practice, these assumptions can result in mothers being identified as the parent accountable for neglectful parenting (any intervention and support then being focused solely on their role). This can raise barriers for effective intervention in practice. Further, the term "failure to protect" is commonly used in statutory practice where there are concerns about abusive, controlling or violent behaviours from a parent within the family, for which a woman is held accountable for not meeting her responsibilities and protecting her child/ren from harm. Daniel and Taylor (2006) suggest that there are three key areas for important consideration:

- the failure to take account of the risks men may pose to children;

- the failure to recognise the benefits that men may offer to children;

- the failure to recognise the pressures on mothers.

HOW CAN WE COLLABORATIVELY IDENTIFY AND RESPOND TO NEGLECT MORE EFFECTIVELY?

The challenges of an effective multi-disciplinary professional network are many. However, a clear and accurate picture of a child's experience of living with neglect will emerge only when information is regularly shared between services (Beesley, 2011) and compiled in an effective way. Hicks and Stein (2010, p. 21, cited by Beesley, 2011, p. 88) set out seven "enablers" of inter-agency working that highlight areas where managers and practitioners should focus:

- understanding and respecting the role and responsibility;

- good communication;

- regular contact and meetings;

- common priorities and trust;

- joint training;

- knowing what services are available and who to contact;

- clear guidelines and procedures for working together.

Working collaboratively with other agencies when responding to child neglect is a challenge. Drawing on the themes identified in this chapter, strategies that help build professional relationships with practitioners in partner organisations and promote information sharing include the following:

Management and strategic staff should:

- Cultivate understanding around the barriers that impede successful inter-agency collaboration.

- Make informal and formal opportunities available to staff to support knowledge development of partner agencies' terms, roles, approaches and methods of working.

- Create opportunities to spend time in partner agencies to develop expertise across services through informal day visits, or formal secondments/co-location of services (with counterparts in universal services).

- Ensure training on child neglect is undertaken in a multi-disciplinary setting.

Practitioners should:

- Spend time getting to know and building trusting working relationships with individuals in partner agencies.

- Actively encourage staff in other services to attend multi-agency meetings.

- Provide regular feedback and communications to staff in universal services about the outcome of their referrals.

- Utilise the local authority's threshold guidance/matrix document as a tool for reflective discussion with colleagues in other disciplines to support knowledge development, inform decision-making and foster a shared language.

(Adapted from Sharley, 2020)

CASE STUDY: DELILAH

Neglect across the life course can have long-term significant impacts for children; it is crucial that as practitioners we can identify neglect and be confident in doing so. It is often a challenge when we work with families where neglect is a long-standing feature and interventions are worked repeatedly with limited impact. There is a need to address neglect holistically and take into account not just the here and now, but to consider the future impact.

Delilah (aged three) lives with her parents; her mother has some learning difficulties and her father has a history of substance misuse and unresolved trauma from when he was a child and experienced neglectful parenting himself. The assessment to date has been undertaken under s.17, child in need; both parents have wanted support for Delilah but in this, multiple worries have become clear. The home conditions are unkempt, dishes are left unwashed and there is limited food, especially fresh food. Delilah is registered with a nursery but her parents struggle to get her to sessions as they have difficulty with the morning routine. There are concerns that the home has smelled of cannabis and cigarette smoke. Delilah's language development is limited and much more in line with a child of 18 months, and there are worries that the TV is used to appease Delilah, and there is limited evidence of stimulation. There are financial concerns and also concern about how this impacts the household as they are at risk of homelessness.

Therefore, the assessment has identified multiple areas of vulnerability, further explored when looking at the family's history, as prior to birth Delilah was subject to a child protection plan for neglect. When Delilah was six months old, it was felt that her home experience no longer met the threshold for child protection and could be supported under child in need. Delilah's case was closed to children's social care six weeks later.

Neglect has been a feature for Delilah since before she was born. By utilising the family history, the context for Delilah changes from an episode of neglect to what is found to be a repeated area of worry. The issues that had reduced have re-emerged, and what became evident is that this resulted in developmental impact, as well as an increased level of social isolation. When discussing the case in supervision, the social worker considers how this level of harm currently is a worry, but without clear planned intervention the level of harm will continue to impact Delilah.

There was consideration given to how best to protect Delilah. A risk assessment was undertaken and a Family Group Conference (FGC) was convened with the aim of supporting the family to identify what support they felt could be implemented to safeguard Delilah. The practitioner, through reflective supervision and by taking a restorative approach, has been considering the context and history to facilitate a support plan with the family that is timely and addresses the risks posed.

Questions:

- Imagine you are Delilah. What would you be thinking?

- How can you try and find out about and understand Delilah's lived experiences?

(Juanita Scallan, independent social worker)

Reflective exercise:

Using the Anti-Poverty Guide produced by BASW, how would you work differently to support Delilah and her mother? (See link below to the Anti-Poverty Guide.)

KEY POINTS FOR PRACTICE

- **Think family:** The effective assessment of child neglect requires a multi-faceted approach. Consider all members of the family in your assessment and the roles they hold in the child/ren's lives. Gather information on the family's history, identify the cross-generational patterns and any unresolved adverse childhood trauma that could impact parenting ability.

- **Time:** The assessment of and intervention in neglect requires time if the support offered is to adequately meet the child/ren's needs. The time taken to assess must also be carefully balanced with the need to intervene to prevent drift or delay occuring. Time is a prerequisite for developing a relationship with a family so that they feel supported to effect positive changes. Time is crucial when planning professional endings when services withdraw from children and families' lives. Careful planning to ensure that other avenues of support are in place is paramount (e.g. family, community, and universal services).

- **Supervision:** Robust supervision is key. Supervision offers the time and space for practitioners to reflect on their observations and experiences, hypothesise, and consider the role that confirmation bias may be playing in their work. Space for discussion with a more senior or experienced colleague to explore a number of options for a child and their family is necessary.

- **Child development:** A sound understanding of child development theory is important. Children may experience neglectful parenting or care as normal. You may need to look closely at the child's circumstances to identify the impact that it is having.

FURTHER READING AND RESOURCES

Websites

Horwath J (no date) *A Day in the Life of...Making sense of an individual's lived experiences*, available at: https://bit.ly/3H1XEwd

NSPCC, The Graded Care Profile 2 Assessment: https://bit.ly/3Wb0Z0v

NSPCC (2022) *Neglect: Learning from case reviews: summary of key issues and learning for improved practice*, available at: https://bit.ly/3kgjrYl

BASW, U*nderstanding Social Work and Poverty*, available at: https://bit.ly/3iGhxQ3

Social Workers Toolbox – The Graded Care Profile Assessment, available at: https://bit.ly/3k7TZUB

Talking and Listening to Children Project (2022), available at: www.talkingandlisteningtochildren.co.uk/

Practice and policy briefings

BASW (2019) *Anti-Poverty Practice Guide for Social Work*, available at: https://bit.ly/3H2Yskz

Lefevre M (2010) *Communicating with Children and Young People: Making a difference* (Social Work in Practice Series), Bristol: Policy Press

Procedures Online (no date) *The Home Conditions Assessment Tool*, available at: https://bit.ly/3XavcOi

Research

Ferguson H (2016) *Making Home Visits: Creativity and the embodied practices of home visiting in social work and child protection*, available at: https://bit.ly/3GF5tGR

Joseph Rowntree Foundation (2016) *The Relationship between Poverty, Child Abuse and Neglect: An evidence review*, available at: https://bit.ly/3k7UpKF

Moran P (2009) *Neglect: Research evidence to inform practice*, available at: https://www.basw.co.uk/system/files/resources/basw_43707-5_0.pdf

Price M (2018) *Enough is Enough: How social workers make judgements when intervening to safeguard neglected children*, available at: https://bit.ly/3vYOlXG

Chapter 5
Responding to neglect – working effectively with other agencies

INTRODUCTION

Although safeguarding and promoting the welfare of children is widely acknowledged as everyone's responsibility (HM Government, 2020), joint working across professional disciplines remains one of the biggest challenges for neglect practice (Pithouse and Crowley, 2016). This chapter focuses on the importance of inter-professional collaboration when responding to children living with neglect, giving particular consideration to the role that staff in schools play. As with many universal services positioned at the heart of the community, schools are crucial safeguarding partners which are able to identify and intervene in neglect at an early point, whilst providing children and families with support and guidance. This chapter considers difficulties that can arise when working with the complexity of neglect across many different organisational boundaries and professional disciplines. It also considers the role of the state as the corporate parent. Drawing on empirical research conducted by Sharley (2018) into the role of schools in identifying and responding to child neglect, the chapter offers a number of emerging themes for interprofessional practice, and suggests a range of strategies that aim to improve interprofessional communication to enhance relationships across services (Sharley, 2018; 2019).

SCHOOLS AS CRUCIAL SAFEGUARDING PARTNERS

Schools, as universal services, support children's cognitive, social and emotional development (Baginsky, 2008). Not only are they sites of learning, but they also offer children and their families access to a range of staff and support services. In fact, staff in schools are recognised as some of the most significant, and often consistent, adults in a child's life who are able to see children five days a week, over an extended period of time and development. Unlike social workers in community teams, school staff have the opportunity to observe children's emotional, cognitive and social development on a daily basis and in a range of classroom and non-classroom settings. The daily visibility of children within the school context and knowledge of their overall health and welfare was absent during the Covid-19 pandemic when schools were closed during periods of national lockdown. Surveillance of children who are home-schooled introduces a challenge, as schools provide sites where children can be observed alongside their peers and in their interactions with their families, whether at school-drop-off, family events, or in school-club settings. As a result, school staff can commonly hold expertise and knowledge about children's home lives and their family's wider functioning. Staff can also possess an acute awareness of the broader contextual safeguarding issues in the local community, particularly for those children who are inadequately supervised outside of the school setting. The relationship between practitioners in statutory services and those within wider universal services that support children can be challenging. The following quote from a teacher demonstrates what can be a commonly held perspective by school staff who have contact with children on a daily basis.

I found the relationship between schools and social services very difficult, in that there's little relationship there. We are with these children for six hours a day or more, five days a week, those children are in our care, yet in my experience we are not called upon or involved as much when there is a social issue.

(Class teacher and governor)

THE ROLE OF SCHOOL STAFF

The role and contribution of school staff in responding to neglect is wide-ranging. Staff in schools and other settings such as early years service providers are involved across the continuum of neglect intervention (Beesley, 2011), from the provision of pastoral support and early help through centre- or school-based services, involvement in child in need (s.17) and child protection provision (s.47), to supporting children who are looked after or adopted (Berridge *et al*, 2021; Welsh Government, 2021a). Staff in universal and education settings have the opportunity to develop relationships with children over time and can gather information and evidence that builds a comprehensive picture of a child's life and the care (or lack of) that they receive.

With persistent cuts to early and preventative local authority budgets and resources, and in the context of continued austerity, early years centres and schools are recognised for the vital, longer term support they provide to families, specifically support offered before and/or after statutory level interventions from the local authority (Sidebotham *et al*, 2016). At individual level, the situated and prolonged nature of interactions with children and their parents can mean that school staff are well placed to possess strong and established relationships with family members. These familiar, formed relationships can offer a solid foundation from which staff and practitioners feel more able to sensitively challenge parents/carers where there are worries about the care being provided (Sharley, 2019).

INTERPROFESSIONAL CHALLENGES

The policy document *Working Together to Safeguard Children* (HM Government, 2018, p.6) asserts that 'practitioners will be clear about what is required of them individually, and how they need to work together in partnership with others'. However, despite this straightforward statement, professional relationships across agencies and disciplines are acknowledged as difficult to navigate, and can be characterised by many challenges. This is further emphasised when responding to child neglect, given its multifaceted nature and conceptual complexity, and the wide range of roles that contribute support along the neglect continuum.

Messages from research

Findings from Sharley's (2018) study, *Identifying and Responding to Child Neglect in Schools*, found a number of important themes that offer messages for inter-professional practice in this area. The mixed methods study comprised of interviews with a range of staff in six primary and secondary schools in Wales and case file analysis of schools' contributions to child protection interventions in three local authorities. The themes that emerged have wider implications and transferable learning to any relationship between practitioners in statutory and other universal settings:

- school staff felt underconfident in their ability to identify child neglect in their roles;

- the existence of rules and routines within the schools strongly govern communication with statutory services;

- a power imbalance exists between schools and statutory social workers;

- school staff focus on the visibility of physical neglect; and

- the professional relationships school staff held with practitioners in social work teams were commonly strained and unproductive.

The next section briefly visits each theme in turn to share the experiences, thoughts and feelings of the school staff who participated in the study.

Lack of staff's professional confidence

Although school staff have regular safeguarding training, in the 30 interviews undertaken, all of the staff reported that the topic of neglect was not covered in their pre-service qualifications, nor had the majority had the opportunity to undertake neglect-specific training since they began their roles. In some schools, this was due to the high demand for training and its limited availability. The absence of training on neglect left staff feeling unprepared to effectively respond to neglect when presented with it in their day-to-day roles. This raises important considerations for interprofessional practice with school staff, particularly given the shifting construction and temporal nature of neglect within societies.

Rules and processes in schools

The strong presence of rules and routines within school culture was an area of considerable discussion during the interviews. School policies and protocols were reported to "simplify" and "speed up" decision-making, easing pressures on their daily roles. Systems were particularly evident in the school setting in relation to safeguarding procedures, where staff reported "passing up" concerns about neglect through designated individuals (such as safeguarding leads) and management hierarchies. Due to these hierarchies, staff felt uneasy about taking any actions outside of their prescribed roles. In instances where staff had serious and significant concerns about a child, staff stressed the importance of sharing information within the school in line with the school's policy, rather than directly with statutory services, even when concerns were significant.

> I will always refer down to the child protection officers and everything will go to those two members of staff. What I've been told is that if you've done that you passed on the duty then to the Child Protection Officer.
>
> (Class teacher)

> I've emailed the Head of Year...just to say my concerns; so I know I have passed that on: and should anything happen to him [child] I've done my bit and that's OK – it's not OK, but I have done what I should do; or feel I should do; because it's not in my power to go any further than that.
>
> (Attendance officer)

Similar findings are identified by Bullock *et al* (2019), who found that teachers and support workers in primary schools did not commonly act on identified neglect, holding the perception that concerns are "not serious enough". Instead, staff had a tendency to favour the gathering and recording of information within the school to build a broader picture of evidence. Whilst the value of processes in large organisations is acknowledged, added layers of administration and systems can risk the effective and timely sharing of information across services. This approach could be linked to the perception that neglect is the lesser form of maltreatment, and/or the perception that a referral to children's services based on worries of neglect alone is seen by some services as unlikely to result in statutory action or intervention (Sharley, 2020).

Power imbalances between staff and social workers

Lessons from case/practice reviews continue to recognise the effect of an imbalance of power in professional relationships, highlighting in particular those that exist between school staff and social work practitioners. These imbalances of power can manifest in some staff or practitioners as not feeling able to challenge professional opinion where differences are held (Sharley, 2019), not sharing relevant information with statutory services in multi-agency meetings (SCIE, 2016a), or not feeling able to share concerns about a child in the presence of their parent/s or carer/s (SCIE, 2016c). In the interviews, staff talked about their tendency to typically defer to the expertise of social workers, holding the view that statutory practitioners have greater status and skills in social care, are authoritative and powerful "agents of the state", and that "going against" the social worker is not a welcomed position. This perspective highlights an important contradiction – from one perspective, staff stated that they felt much better positioned in terms of their knowledge about children and their care within families due to the daily contact they have, but from another, they felt they lacked the confidence to professionally challenge the views of social workers if these were to contradict their own professional opinions.

A focus on physical neglect

Staff also talked about being principally drawn to observing the presentation of children when looking to recognise neglect, rather than gathering information from a combination of other less obvious indicators (e.g. emotional, medical, educational or supervisory concerns). That said, a few of the school staff interviewed reported giving attention to children's demeanours, the way they communicated and their body language. This is an important point to consider for interprofessional practice – the focus on physical neglect – and how some school staff may understand and notice neglect. A strong theme in the findings of the study was staff's desire to monitor children whom they were concerned about with the purpose of building a detailed picture over a period of time. Davies and Ward (2012) suggest that this approach can often be taken to gather evidence to legitimise an organisation's decision to refer to statutory services. In the interviews, school staff were clear that they found their worries about neglect harder to prove than other forms of maltreatment, when they are "smaller issues" "bubbling along the bottom", with their constructions of neglect differing from those of practitioners in statutory services. Staff believed that referrals that cited neglect alone were less likely to receive statutory intervention, compared to those that included tangible evidence of physical, sexual or emotional abuse (Sharley, 2019).

> *...they are the small issues – we get things like concerns about dirty ears, children saying they haven't had breakfast, packed lunches are small, head lice is a big one. We get things like that you can't identify straight away as a kind of abuse. Physical [neglect] is quite easy, but these things are bubbling along the bottom.*
>
> (Deputy head teacher and safeguarding lead)

Professional relationships

Communication between school staff and social workers or social work teams was emphasised as a significant barrier to the sharing of information with statutory services. Differences in professional language, (lack of) knowledge of intervention thresholds, and definitions of neglect brought challenges in the transmission of information. Staff talked about the impact of the social work profession's recruitment and retention problem on their professional relationships with children's services, and the frustration they felt at not being able to make contact and get updates or advice on case developments when the allocated worker was absent or frequently changed. This made sharing information about the child's daily lived experiences challenging. The lack of professional consistency was identified as weakening the effectiveness of their inter-professional relationships – which remains one of the biggest challenges encountered in work with child neglect (Haynes, 2015). A lack of feedback shared with schools on referrals made was cited as a common frustration, specifically when referrals were returned after long delays with "no case to answer" with no explanation as to why. The absence of communication from statutory services perpetuated school staff's inability to understand the rationale for the decision taken.

> *Sometimes you think, 'Well I wasn't expecting that to come back again', and then you refer another one with more detail and you think 'Well that's OK, that one I've covered every angle there' and it bounces back!*
>
> (Teaching assistant)

That's one of the criticisms...we don't get feedback on referrals. We only get feedback if they're picking it up. We don't get the letter to say 'Thanks very much for your referral, but on this occasion we're not [intervening].'

(I lead of inclusion)

HOW CAN WE WORK MORE EFFECTIVELY ACROSS SERVICES?

The challenges of an effective and successful professional network are many. However, a clear and accurate picture of a child's experience of living with neglect will only emerge when information is regularly shared between services (Beesley, 2011) and compiled in a clear and organised way. Hicks and Stein (2010, p. 21, cited by Beesley, 2011, p. 88) set out seven "enablers" of inter-agency working that highlight areas where managers and practitioners should focus:

- understanding and respecting the role and responsibility;

- good communication;

- regular contact and meetings;

- common priorities and trust;

- joint training;

- knowing what services are available and who to contact;

- clear guidelines and procedures for working together.

Working collaboratively with other agencies when responding to child neglect is a challenge. In March 2021, the What Works for Children's Social Care Centre confirmed £12.6 million from the DfE to run and evaluate programmes to improve the safeguarding and educational outcomes for children with a social worker, involving 21 local authorities in England (WWCSC, 2022). This funding extends the Social Workers in Schools project to understand if placing social workers in schools can facilitate better relationships between social workers, schools and families to improve outcomes.

Drawing on the themes identified in this chapter, strategies that help build professional relationships with practitioners in partner organisations and promote the sharing of information consistent with the regulator's Professional Standards for Social Workers (3.6, 3.7) (Social Work England, 2019) include those set out below.

Management and strategic staff should:

- Cultivate understanding around the barriers which impede successful inter-agency collaboration.

- Make informal and formal opportunities available to staff to support knowledge development of partner agencies' terms, roles, approaches and methods of working.

- Create opportunities to spend time in partner agencies to develop expertise across services through informal day visits, or formal secondments/co-location of services (with counterparts in universal services).

- Ensure training on child neglect is undertaken in a multi-disciplinary setting.

Practitioners should:

- Spend time getting to know and building trusting working relationships with individuals in partner agencies.

- Actively encourage staff in other services to attend multi-agency meetings.

- Provide regular feedback and communications to staff in universal services about the outcome of their referrals.

- Utilise the local authority's threshold guidance/matrix document as a tool for reflective discussion with colleagues in other disciplines to support knowledge development, inform decision-making and foster a shared language.

(Adapted from Sharley, 2020)

CASE STUDY: EMMA

Emma (aged six) has been known to children's services since prior to birth. She is one of five children and the second eldest child in the family. Concerns have been intermittent and centred around neglect, poor home conditions, parental substance misuse, and parental mental health. Concerns have included Emma's mother's lack of engagement with services, including housing, education and health. Emma's attendance at school has been limited, which has impacted her development, ability to build positive relationships and the opportunity to experience similar things to her peers. Emma has been subject to a child protection plan for nine months.

In usual times, family support services would have actively supported the family to address many of these concerns. However, without their involvement (due to the Covid-19 pandemic), and the limited changes Emma's mother has made, there are worries around the children's needs not being adequately met. The interventions and support offered are not giving professionals the assurance that the children's experience is improving, though the family view is that the situation is better and they are trying to make improvements, as they love the children and want what is best for them. Most significantly, despite substantial support, during lockdown Emma has not been attending the remote learning provided by the school, which has impacted her education and social interaction. Since the school has recently reopened and face-to-face learning has resumed, Emma is now regularly attending school. However, the concerns for her overall care and welfare remain.

Emma's class teacher calls children's services to inform them about her concerns. The teacher feels worried about Emma as she came to school today with a dirty jumper and a visible tide mark around her neck. In the conversation, she also tells you that Emma has been withdrawn and unhappy in lessons and seems very reluctant to go home after school. She wishes you to look into this, but doesn't want you to tell the family that she has contacted you as she says she has a good working relationship with Emma's mother and does not want to jeopardise this now that Emma is back at school.

(Juanita Scallan, independent social worker)

Questions:

- What do you do and why?

- What are the challenges for interprofessional relationships with colleagues in schools?

- What legislative, ethical and professional duties around interprofessional practice guide your approach with the teacher?

- How can you encourage and support the open sharing of information by professionals in universal services with parents?

Reflective exercise:

Using your local authority's published threshold document, discuss a referral made to children's services by a partner agency where there are concerns that a child is living with neglect. Through discussion with the practitioner in the partner agency, identify the concerns that have been shared and connect these to levels on the threshold document. Discuss what informed the practitioner's decision to refer to statutory services, and what level of intervention the local authority considers appropriate to meet the child's identified needs.

Can the information contained in the review made by the partner agency be more clearly articulated following the interprofessional/agency discussion?

Is the outcome for the child and their family any different than it was prior to the discussion applying the threshold document?

PRACTITIONER TIPS

- **Curiosity:** Be curious, and ask questions of yourself and of other professionals. What is the experience in the home? If I was the child concerned, what would that feel like?

- **Observe:** When observing, do not focus only on how parents respond to their children, look at how the children also respond to their parents. Is this interaction natural? Would you expect something different?

- **Triangulate:** Effective assessment practice demands information from a range of sources and positions. Ensure that information included in the assessment is verified and analysed. What does it mean for the child?

- **Chronologies:** Compilation of chronologies is crucial in circumstances of neglect. Use a multi-agency approach, look at patterns in the information over weeks, months and years; are there similarities? What interventions have been attempted? How many times? What has worked/not worked? Are interventions being repeated? Will your response now risk causing further drift or delay?

FURTHER READING AND RESOURCES

Websites

Achievement For All (2021) *The Whole School CLA Approach*, available at: https://bit.ly/3Xn1uFJ

National Association of Virtual School Heads (2021) *Promoting the Education of Looked After Children*, available at: https://navsh.org.uk/

SCIE (2016a) *Incomplete Information Sharing by Schools in Child Protection Conferences*, available at: https://bit.ly/3IEoSKN

SCIE (2016b) *Unfocused Discussion in Child Protection Conferences*, available at: https://bit.ly/3GAgOb9

SCIE (2016c) *Reluctance to Share Information in Front of Families in Child Protection Conferences*, available at: https://bit.ly/3ivhFC5

Practice and policy briefings

Berridge D, Sebba J, Cartwright M and Staples E (2021) *Children in Need and Children in Care: Educational Attainment and Progress*, Policy Briefing, Bristol: PolicyBristol, available at: https://bit.ly/3H1sntz

Sharley V (2020) *Responding to Child Neglect in Schools: Messages for inter-agency safeguarding practice*, Policy Briefing, Bristol: PolicyBristol, available at: https://bit.ly/3GVLuFh

Sharley V (2022) 'Responding to child neglect in schools: factors which scaffold safeguarding practice for staff in mainstream education in Wales', *Research Papers in Education*, available at: https://bit.ly/3mYLgWR

Research

Sharley V (2019) 'Identifying and responding to child neglect in schools: differing perspectives and the implications for inter-agency practice', *Child Indicators Research*, 13, pp. 551–571

Chapter 6
Adverse childhood experiences

INTRODUCTION

This chapter considers adverse childhood experiences (ACEs) (also mentioned earlier in Chapter 3), and some of the compounding factors and causes of negative childhood events associated with child neglect. The chapter critically reviews ACEs and considers how thinking about these might guide service delivery, and practice with children. The chapter goes on to look at trauma and a trauma-informed approach when working with children who have experienced neglect, also considering trauma within state care. Lastly, it considers older children who have experienced neglect, clearly highlighting the need for ongoing support.

ADVERSE CHILDHOOD EXPERIENCES

There has been much discussion in recent years of adverse childhood experiences, known as ACEs (Bellis *et al*, 2016). Safe, nurturing relationships and environments underpin children's health and well-being. For children who have been neglected, they are not likely to have always experienced these types of relationships or may not have been in nurturing environments. Living in homes where there is much conflict and large amounts of uncertainty, where children's needs are not considered or prioritised, can cause chronic stress for children. Chronic stress is thought to have a long-term impact on children's health and well-being.

Examples of factors that are seen as adverse childhood experiences are:

- neglect, physical and sexual abuse;

- having parents who are dependent on drugs and/or alcohol and whose focus has not always been on their children, often leaving them unsupervised;

- families where there is domestic abuse and children are "walking on eggshells" because of the fear of escalation, and parents are thus not focused on children's needs;

- families where the parents have been in prison and unable to care for their children, where the children may go and live with unsatisfactory caregivers; and

- families where parents have serious mental health difficulties and cannot focus fully on their children.

All of these adverse experiences are likely to include some degree of neglect of children.

In Wales, a study of 2,000 adults between the ages of 18–69 asked them about their childhood experiences and current health and lifestyle as adults (Bellis *et al*, 2016). This study and numerous others have shown that negative childhood experiences can lead to poorer outcomes in later life with regard to health and emotional well-being (Crouch *et al*, 2020), including development of mental health difficulties, cancer, heart disease, diabetes and premature death (Bellis *et al*, 2016).

The difficulty with ACEs and these kinds of studies is that they are not able to give weightings to each different adverse experience, or measure how significant each difficulty was for an individual child. This means that ACEs can be seen as a simplistic and blunt instrument that cannot necessarily help us to understand individual circumstances. The concept is that stressful experiences damage neurological pathways and cognitive development (also discussed in Chapter 3), leading to poor choices being made in later life, for example, poor diet, smoking, unstable employment, and impulsive or violent behaviour. However, ACEs can be seen as deterministic in assuming that children cannot recover from neglect and their difficult early start in life, and further that the course of their lives is set because of these factors.

Because the concept of ACEs is simplistic, it is easily understood and widely accepted, and many practitioners embrace them as a way of understanding how people's later lifestyle choices are related to their early formative experiences. ACEs can be used in this way to plan and tailor interventions and support. But practitioners also need to consider the impact of self-determination, resilience, subsequent positive experiences with foster carers and adopters of therapeutic parenting (discussed in Chapters 8 and 9), or indeed of fulfilling, mutually affirming adult relationships. We discuss issues of resilience later in this chapter and again in Chapter 9.

The ACEs approach suggests the need to eliminate or reduce the impact of adverse childhood experience to break the cycle of intergenerational adversity, whereby adverse experiences cascade down through the generations. In this way, it is assumed that children who have negative experiences go on to make poor choices and subject their own children to similar difficulties. However, what the concept of ACEs does not fully recognise is that many adult "choices" about diet, smoking and employment are often more related to structural inequalities brought about by poverty, poor education, limited social capital, and poor housing (NHS Highland, 2018), all of which are closely related to neglect (see Chapter 4).

In an attempt to ameliorate or eliminate ACEs, strategies and workforce priorities might include, for example:

- strengthening economic support for families (tax credits, family-friendly policies);

- promoting social norms that protect against violence and adversity, for example, public education campaigns and education in schools about respectful and equitable relationships;

- focusing on early years support for young children, for example, family hubs and initiatives like Sure Start programmes;

- increasing parenting skills to help parents and young people handle stress and everyday challenges, for example, healthy relationship programmes;

- building resilience in young people (by linking them to mentoring schemes and sources of support in the community);

- therapeutic parenting and trauma-informed approaches.

All of these streams of work would aim to minimise ACEs and child neglect (NCIPC, 2019).

Despite advising a cautionary approach to ACEs, there have been some moves to incorporate a more nuanced understanding of the interface of societal, parental and household factors, an individual's experience of trauma, what triggers a memory of it, combined with an understanding of how best to respond (see *Annual Report of Director for Public Health, NHS Highland*, 2018, p. 14). This is detailed in the following diagram:

Interlocking risk factors

Social/societal factors
- Poverty
- Unemployment
- Deprivation
- Social isolation

Household factors
- Domestic violence
- Problem substance use
- Mental ill health
- Separation
- Living in care

Family/parental factors
- Parenting skills
- Parenting capacity
- Parental age
- Family structure

Intergenerational factors
- Violence
- Parent ACE exposure
- Inequalities

(Taken from NHS Highland, 2018, p. 14)

A range of strategies have been developed to help mitigate against the harms of ACEs for those who have already experienced some negative life events in childhood and the resulting trauma, one of which is a trauma-informed approach (Levenson, 2017).

A TRAUMA-INFORMED APPROACH

Practitioners need to adopt a therapeutic and thoughtful response that embeds the child in the present but takes account of their past experiences (Levenson, 2017). Children who are traumatised by neglect and abuse are often seen to adopt one of three responses – flight, fright or freeze. Children who have experienced trauma can also become what many describe as hyper-vigilant, always on the alert for danger, and can sometimes react in a way that may seem out of proportion to the challenge or difficulty (Golding and Hughes, 2012). Workers, carers and parents can work to ameliorate traumatic experiences by helping children to understand what is happening to them, and helping to increase children and young people's sense of control and resilience. There is an increasing emphasis on understanding the neurobiology of trauma (as also discussed in relation to ACEs) and changes in the brain that can cause children to be constantly anxious and hyper-vigilant (Golding and Hughes, 2012) (see also Chapter 3). Affected children can behave in ways over which they have no conscious control. This can be frightening and challenging for both children and their carers.

Traumatic memories of neglect are stored in the brain differently to everyday memories, and are remembered in vivid images and sensations (ISP Fostering, 2021). Traumatic memories can flood a child's mind when triggered by sights, smells, sounds or reminders. Feelings of terror and helplessness return, reinforcing to the child that they are incapable, unworthy or not valued. When beginning to understand a child who is placed in foster care or being adopted, recognising their past experiences of neglect, the triggers and likely impact is helpful, as is guiding the child to recognise their own responses.

CASE STUDY: KYLE

Kyle is seven years old. He has previously experienced very high levels of neglect, fighting constantly for food. Kyle's foster carer, Pete, tells me how Kyle had become anxious the evening before, just after they'd taken the dogs for a walk. One of the dogs had got quite boisterous and Pete had had to tell the dog off. Pete then told me about the tricky morning he'd just had. Kyle had woken much earlier than usual and immediately started calling out. When Paul had come into the bedroom, Kyle had hidden under the bed and refused to come out, all the time shouting, sobbing and swearing.

Eventually, Kyle was coaxed out from under the bed, now trying to slap Paul. As he calmed and while Paul helped him to dress, Kyle acted out how his mother used to treat him, locking him in his room and not letting him eat. He'd talked about this many times before, but Paul still patiently listened, knowing that carefully listening to Kyle's story was part of the trauma-informed healing process.

But this time the story was different. This time, Kyle said that they had a dog and that his mother would always feed the dog first, even if Kyle hadn't been allowed food all day. He told Paul that sometimes his mother would get the dog to bark at him and that he'd cry. When he cried, he had to stand in the corner of the room. He now likes it when the dogs are told off, but he also loves the dogs. He'd been thinking about them all night.

> Using a trauma-informed perspective, Paul reflected on the effects of previous neglect and of how Kyle's behaviours had masked his trauma. If he'd only looked at Kyle's behaviour, he'd have seen a naughty boy, whereas looking at Kyle's behaviour through a trauma lens revealed a little boy who was treated second to the family dog.
>
> (Dave Walker, psychotherapist, fostering support agency, South Wales)

TRAUMA IN THE CARE SYSTEM

Trauma-informed work highlights the importance of emotional and physical safety, and creating opportunities to rebuild a sense of control and empowerment (DeCandia and Guarino, 2015). This approach also involves anticipating and avoiding individual and organisational practices that could retraumatise the child (Furnivall and Grant, 2014).

If we think of the care system as a whole, there are a number of significant life-changing situations that can have retraumatising impacts on children, for example, regularly moving foster home, changing schools (Mannay *et al*, 2017), and moving into residential care (UK Fostering, 2022). Each of these can create hugely stressful situations that those children who are not in care rarely face. Institutional practices have not always helped, for example, black bags have often been used for packing children's belongings during these moves, which can be degrading and humiliating in that it denotes a lack of value of the child.

Further opportunities for recurring trauma can also occur when children are leaving the care system and around the anxiety this may pose. Children and young people are expected to exit from the care system and be independent much earlier than most young people (not in care) would be expected to move away from their families. Whilst young people are usually supervised by leaving care teams and supported by a local authority personal adviser to plan their pathway to independence, children can find themselves without education or employment and moved into unsuitable accommodation or indeed homeless (The Prince's Trust, 2017; Sheen, 2022). It is vital that young people are supported through this major life transition. A helpful guide to care leavers' rights and entitlements is available from Coram Voice, 2020 (see resources at the end of the chapter).

Some children also experience neglect and abuse in foster care, residential care or adoption. In 2009, in an analysis of 173 serious case reviews, 17 were in relation to children in care or adopted from care (Ofsted, 2009). Whilst neglect was not identified by itself, six major themes emerged from a later review of serious case reviews (Beesley, 2011, pp. 10–102):

- insufficient focus on children's needs (children are rarely listened to);

- lack of rigour in assessing foster carers and adopters;

- poor multi-agency working and information sharing;

- lack of compliance with statutory requirements;

- omissions in staff training.

Rees *et al* (2021a and b) found similar themes in their review of child practice reviews in Wales with regard to children not being listened to, children rarely being seen alone, and the need to consider the child's lived experience (see also Chapters 4 and 5). Thus, we can see how important it is that we are closely attuned to children's needs, ensure we see children alone, and listen to their feelings. The Talking and Listening to Children Project (TLC) has created a series of online resources to help practitioners improve their communication skills with children (see resources at the end of this chapter).

Children who have been neglected may have a distrust of adults who have not protected or provided for them, and this might be one of the reasons why children can potentially misinterpret the intentions of those who work with and care for them (Sinclair *et al*, 2004; The Fostering Network, 2022). It is important that we regularly communicate with children to help them discuss their concerns.

AVOIDING RE-TRAUMATISATION

Given that children can be subject to re-traumatisation, it is important that they are given as much information as possible about moves of home and school, so that they have time to discuss and prepare. Disruption of routines can be particularly upsetting for children who have experienced neglect and trauma. Clear rules and routines can be helpful (Naish, 2018), especially at times of transition. When change is about to happen, even as small as going on holiday, or more significant like changing schools, explaining and discussing what and how things will be different is important, so children can be assured their needs are going to be catered for. When a disruption is unexpected, adults may need to support children to keep calm. Expecting any child to move foster home at short notice is perhaps not surprisingly going to cause extreme upset and fear, and particularly for someone who has experienced previous disruption, trauma and years of neglect.

When children are being looked after by the state, it is vital that practitioners are alert to signs of emotional rejection, including the child being treated differently or worse than others in the same foster home. For example, this could be being expected to eat in a separate room, or eat different or inferior foods to the foster carer's own children.

It may be that for a child who has experienced neglect, anything that appears as being treated differently, overlooked or ignored can be interpreted as rejection, which can remind the child of their past experiences, reinforcing their image of themselves as unworthy, unloved or unlovable. Carers or workers need to provide a sense of availability, warmth and reliability for the child to help them feel more secure (see also the section on the Secure Base in Chapter 8). Children may need support in recognising their own and others' emotions without feeling overwhelmed or ashamed. It is helpful for children to learn about the impact trauma caused by neglect has had on their lives and for practitioners to talk to them about this.

Good practice might mean working with a child to develop a list of key events or anniversaries that could be particularly difficult to navigate. In addition, working with the child to list things, even times of day, or situations that make them anxious or scared will be helpful, so they can begin to be able to anticipate and prepare for such eventualities. This could be shared with school staff, for example, so significant adults can work together to try to avoid practices that might be retraumatising. Parents' evenings may hold particular significance, where parents have failed to attend in the past. Multi-disciplinary working is essential (see also Chapter 5), so that everyone working with the child takes a similar approach. Significant adults need to be alert to signs of arousal or anxiety in a child. Anticipating and intervening early is helpful to both recognise and manage distress and can help strengthen a child's capacity to exert control over their responses (Furnivall and Grant, 2014).

The Whole School Approach

The Whole School Approach is a case example of a universal adoption of a trauma-informed model. It is an ACE- and trauma-informed programme that has been developed across Wales to introduce and implement good practice to improve emotional and mental well-being for all children within schools. Chapter 5 emphasises the crucial role schools have in supporting children who are living with or experiencing neglect, and the importance of working collaboratively with all members of school staff. There are four elements to this approach (Welsh Government, 2021b):

- an ACE readiness tool developed to identify existing provisions in school and gaps that may impede the adoption of an ACE-informed approach;

- staff training to improve the awareness, knowledge and skills of all school staff when working with children affected by trauma;

- a school action plan; and

- a resource pack to provide additional support needed to embed and sustain an ACE-informed approach.

See the resources list at the end of this chapter.

The ACE-informed Whole School Approach was initially piloted in three primary schools in Wales, within the Maesteg area of Bridgend County Borough Council between September and December 2017 (Welsh Government, 2021b). An independent evaluation of the pilot was conducted by Public Health Wales to develop an understanding of how well the approach has been adopted into everyday practice. This evaluation highlighted that addressing children's well-being is considered essential to the academic success of pupils and that tackling the effects of ACEs is "everybody's problem". The approach was subsequently adopted across Wales, and children's well-being now constitutes 25 per cent of the curriculum. This approach aims to sensitise education staff to trauma, abuse and neglect.

WORKING WITH OLDER CHILDREN

Having discussed the impact that trauma from neglect can have, and how practitioners and carers might take a trauma-informed approach to help children, we now consider working with older children (also covered in Chapter 3 in terms of identifying neglect in adolescence). Both fostering and adopting older children can be seen to be more difficult, because children may have cumulatively experienced more neglect, trauma and disruption; and for many adopters in particular, they are often more reluctant to adopt older children (Palmer et al, 2023). When children are adopted, there is an assumption that the family will become a self-contained, independent, "ordinary" family who do not require additional support. Kempenaar (former Chair of the Wales Advisory Group of Adoption) undertook a PhD study into adoption support (2015) and found that when applying to adopt, although an adoption support plan is created, adopters did not feel able, or are often not encouraged, to identify any support needs, in case they were seen as being less attractive as adopters. Thus, when an adoption placement is made, it can be difficult for any meaningful support plan to be in place, and adopters may find it difficult to ask for help. It is important that adopters have access to available information, strategies, resources and support. For some children fostered or adopted, despite long periods of stability, therapeutic approaches to parenting (see Chapter 8 and 9) and nurturing by the foster carers or adopters, difficulties and trauma may recur or develop later on. Selwyn *et al* (2015) studied adoptive families and found that the average age of a child at the point of disruption was 13 years, and the majority of disrupted adoptions had been in place for more than five years. This suggests that difficulties caused by the impact of previous neglect and abuse can continue or be triggered and re-emerge when a child reaches adolescence. We know that adolescence is a challenging period for all young people who struggle to understand their identity and forge more independence. In the Selwyn study, of the placements that broke down, 94 per cent of the children had experienced neglect by their birth family. In interviews with adopters, they often used the word trauma to describe the impact on the child of their early life experiences. Support for adopters was found to be lacking; all adoption managers thought the adoption support plans should be improved, and access to support should be more readily forthcoming (Selwyn *et al*, 2015). Thus, we can see the impact of trauma continues and/or recurs in adolescence and there is a need for an ongoing trauma-informed approach. This suggests that continued support should be provided to both adopters and foster carers and the young people in their care to help facilitate a healthy transition to adulthood.

CONCLUSION

The range of identified adverse childhood experiences all closely link to child neglect. The ACEs perspective is very popular but should be approached with caution, as it does not help to gauge the relative weighting of the various difficulties a child has experienced; it does not help us understand individual circumstances; and we cannot assume that a child who has been neglected will necessarily encounter more difficulties in later life. Children often experience trauma as a result of neglect. A trauma-informed approach is a helpful way to understand children's behaviour as a response to their previous experiences of neglect. Listening to children and working to understand the triggers is a useful way to help children begin to manage their responses and behaviour.

Children may experience long periods of stability, but difficulties may recur, especially around adolescence, and ongoing support may be required. Whilst a trauma-informed approach is focused on the negative events that have happened to a child, it is also important to focus on children's strengths and abilities; how foster carers or adopters might do this is discussed further in Chapter 8. Much research has focused on poor outcomes for looked after children, yet many go on to lead very fulfilling and successful lives, and positive care-experienced role models should be highlighted to children, so they can envision a positive future for themselves (Taussig *et al*, 2021; Sissay 2022). It is important to recognise that children traumatised by neglect can recover and become productive, successful and supportive citizens (Furnivall and Grant, 2014).

PRACTITIONER TIPS

- Take a cautious approach to ACEs – try to understand individual experiences and what might be triggers for the child.

- Be curious about children's behaviour.

- Consider links to children's previous experiences and their current behaviour.

- Explore feelings with children and listen to them re-telling their story.

- Try to identify triggers.

- Discuss triggers with children to help them manage their behaviour.

- Aim to develop a trauma plan for each child you work with.

- Be prepared for difficulties to recur around adolescence.

- Focus on strengths and resilience and believe that children who have experienced neglect can become productive and caring adults.

FURTHER READING AND RESOURCES

Coram Voice (2020) *Sorted and Supported: A guide to care leavers rights and entitlements*, available at: https://bit.ly/3GZmQ6D

Sheen M (2022) *Lifting the Lid on the Care System*, available at: https://bit.ly/3QwR7Np

Barton E and Newbury A (2018) *An Evaluation of the Adverse Childhood Experience (ACE) –Informed Whole School Approach,* available at: https://bit.ly/3XgEhVE

National Centre for Injury Prevention and Control (2019) *Preventing Adverse Childhood Experiences: Leveraging the best available evidence*, Atlanta, GA: National Center for Injury Prevention and Control, available at: https://www.cdc.gov/violenceprevention/pdf/preventingACES.pdf

Sissay L (2022) 'Every one of us has a different story: a historic portrait of care system success', *The Guardian*, available at: https://bit.ly/3GZHXG3

Practice and policy briefings

ISP Fostering (2021) *How Trauma impacts a Child's Brain*, available at: https://ispfostering.org.uk/childhood-trauma-brain-development/

NHS Highland (2018) *Annual Report of the Director of Public Health 2018, Adverse Childhood Experiences, Resilience and Trauma-Informed Care: A public health approach to understanding and responding to adversity*, available at: https://bit.ly/3IJ4AzJ

Ofsted (2018) *Growing up Neglected: A multi-agency response to older children*, available at: https://bit.ly/2miLoNO

Chapter 7
Child exploitation

INTRODUCTION

This chapter considers both child sexual and criminal exploitation and the relationship to children who have experienced neglect. We start by considering the links between neglect and exploitation and possible signs of exploitation. We then look at definitions of sexual abuse, grooming and misconceptions, before moving on to criminal exploitation. We also consider a contextual safeguarding approach.

WHAT IS THE LINK BETWEEN NEGLECT AND CHILD SEXUAL AND CRIMINAL EXPLOITATION?

The impact of neglect can increase young people's vulnerability to harm from sexual exploitation. Risk factors relate to having experience of neglect or abuse (IISCA, 2022), social isolation, homelessness, having a physical or learning disability, and being in care, especially for those in residential care.

There are several ways in which neglect links to child sexual and criminal exploitation. Birth parents who have less oversight of their children may allow them to spend a lot of time out of home unsupervised, and they are thus more accessible and easier targets for those who seek to exploit them. Similarly, less oversight might mean unfettered access to the internet, which can place children at higher risk. Because neglect can be associated with families in chaos, crisis and need (Taylor and Daniel, 2006), some perpetrators may target such families via a relationship with the child's mother, with the purpose of accessing the children. Perpetrators are known to target places where they know vulnerable children live, for example, children's homes, where many of the children are likely to have experienced abuse and neglect and may not be closely monitored. Children who have experienced neglect are likely to have poor attachment to their caregivers (see Chapters 2 and 5) and may find it difficult to understand nurturing relationships, reciprocity and affection, and be seeking love and acceptance outside the home. Perpetrators will try to further damage family relationships to isolate the child and make them more vulnerable to exploitation.

Children who have been neglected may have feelings of insecurity, unworthiness and low self-esteem, and therefore be more susceptible to attention and reassurance that perpetrators would seemingly offer. They may seek physical contact and comfort that have often been lacking in the home and may be more willing to take risks. In addition, children who have been neglected may also have limited self-efficacy to seek help when needed. Younger children who are neglected can be exposed to pornography or to adults engaging in sexual activity whilst children are present. Children who have disabilities, especially learning difficulties (May-Chahal and Palmer, 2018) or who are non-verbal can be more vulnerable to being targeted.

DEFINITION OF CHILD SEXUAL EXPLOITATION

The most recent definition of child sexual exploitation from the DfE (2017, p. 3) states:

Child sexual exploitation is a form of child sexual abuse. It occurs where an individual or group takes advantage of an imbalance of power to coerce, manipulate or deceive a child or young person under the age of 18 into sexual activity (a) in exchange for something the victim needs or wants, and/or (b) for the financial advantage or increased status of the perpetrator or facilitator. The victim may have been sexually exploited even if the sexual activity appears consensual. Child sexual exploitation does not always involve physical contact; it can also occur through the use of technology.

Like all forms of sexual abuse, child sexual exploitation:

- can affect any child or young person (male or female) under the age of 18 years, including 16- and 17-year-olds who can legally consent to have sex;

- can still be abuse even if the sexual activity appears consensual;

- can include contact (penetrative and non-penetrative acts) and non-contact sexual activity;

- can take place in person or via technology, or a combination of both;

- can involve force and/or enticement-based methods of compliance and may or may not be accompanied by violence or threats of violence;

- may occur without the child or young person's immediate knowledge (through others copying videos or images they have created and posting on social media, for example);

- can be perpetrated by individuals or groups, males or females, and children or adults.

The abuse can be a one-off occurrence or a series of incidents over time, and range from opportunistic to complex organised abuse, and is typified by some form of power imbalance in favour of those perpetrating the abuse. Whilst age may be the most obvious factor, the power imbalance can also be due to a range of other factors, including gender, sexual identity, cognitive ability, physical strength, status, and access to economic or other resources (DfE, 2017).

Children and young people in exploitative situations and relationships are persuaded or forced to perform activities in return for gifts, drugs, money or affection (NSPCC, 2021d). Abusers are not always abusive immediately, and usually undertake a grooming process (Fursland, 2017).

GROOMING

Initially, the abuser locates and targets the child (usually a vulnerable child – a child who has experience of neglect may be an easy target). Perpetrators do this by spending time outside schools, shopping centres, children's homes, etc, where children are not being monitored. Having identified the child, the abuser tends to use a range of tactics, following the stages as set out below:

Flatter
Complimenting, flirting, professing to love the child (the neglected child may feel unlovable and therefore be more susceptible)

↓

Build trust
Become "boyfriend" or partner, offer to resolve problems, offer food, cigarettes, clothing, protect

↓

Normalise sexual activity
Make sexual jokes, talk about sex, expose to pornography (the neglected child may have little understanding of acceptable physical comfort)

Disorientate
Alcohol, drugs (the child who has experienced neglect may feel unhappy and want a release from feelings), switch from being nice to angry, and back again

Intimidate
Threat, slap, insult

Sexual abuse
Once suitably groomed, abuse commences, either by individual or group

(Taken from Fursland, 2017, pp. 11–12)

As well as grooming, abusers can draw children into exploitation via what is known as the party model.

Party model

Child sexual exploitation can start via peer-to-peer contact and involve attendance at parties set up for this specific purpose, known as the "party model" (Fursland, 2017). The child who has experienced neglect may be under-confident and have difficulty making friends, and be keen to join in and gain status among peers. As with grooming, alcohol, drugs and food are supplied for free as an incentive to attend (alcohol and drugs may be more of an incentive for children who wish to block out memories of their past experiences) and then young people become part of an "in-group". Later, they are told they are in debt for the drugs, alcohol or clothing received and are expected to repay via sexual favours. Young people find it difficult to extricate themselves from this "debt bondage" arrangement and are put under huge amounts of pressure to remain involved, including threats to themselves, their friends and/or family.

Misconceptions

Welsh Government commissioned a review of current policy (Hallett *et al*, 2017) and found that whilst there is an increasing awareness of child sexual exploitation by professionals, carers and the public, there is evidence to suggest that some common misconceptions and misunderstandings around child sexual exploitation remain. In particular, misconceptions often relate the wrongful assumptions that:

- boys are not likely to be targeted;

- women cannot be abusers;

- children are responsible by "consenting" to abuse, even though they are being manipulated and threatened by adults;

- young people and peers cannot be abusers; and that

- sexual exploitation only happens in certain ethnic communities.

  Child sexual exploitation can occur in all of these ways, and it is important that practitioners and carers are aware of this, and especially alert to any signs in young people who have experienced neglect.

DEFINITION OF CHILD CRIMINAL EXPLOITATION

Criminal exploitation is child abuse where children and young people are coerced and manipulated into committing crimes (NSPCC, 2021d). It is similar to sexual exploitation, although the child is utilised not for sexual but for financial gain (although child sexual abuse is also often associated with financial gain, where perpetrators charge others for abusing children). A child may be both sexually and criminally exploited at the same time. The grooming process is very similar and is often organised by groups of people, usually men, operating in gangs who target vulnerable children such as those who have experienced neglect. The grooming process involves offering the young people status items, which they could not ordinarily afford, such as designer trainers or clothing, which might be more appealing to children who have insufficient or inferior clothing, as is likely for a child experiencing neglect. The "party model" is often a way of bringing children into criminal exploitation, by providing cannabis and a variety of other drugs and alcohol. The young people then become indebted to those who provided the goods or drugs and are expected to repay this debt. This repayment can range from being required to shoplift across geographical boundaries, to carrying and supplying drugs. As already highlighted, these operations are usually managed by gangs, for example, those involved in "county lines". The 2018 Home Office Serious

Violence Strategy provides a definition of a county line as a term used to describe:

> *...gangs and organised criminal networks involved in exporting illegal drugs into one or more importing areas [within the UK], using dedicated mobile phone lines or other form of "deal line". They are likely to exploit vulnerable children to move [and store] the drugs and money and they will often use coercion, intimidation, violence (including sexual violence) and weapons.*

(See National Crime Agency resource at the end of this chapter.) Children are in some instances trafficked to areas a long way from home as part of the network's drug-dealing business. As is the case in child sexual exploitation, children often do not recognise themselves as victims, nor do they realise they have been groomed to become involved in criminality. The young person who has experienced neglect may have less confidence and agency to try and avoid or extricate themselves from such situations (see section on trauma-informed work in Chapter 6). It is important that practitioners understand the role perpetrators play, and support children in these circumstances. Once enmeshed, it is extremely difficult to disengage or leave the gang. This can leave carers, family members and social workers at a loss as to how to help.

We can see that children who have been neglected may be targeted because of their vulnerability. There are a range of factors linking child neglect to child exploitation. However, it is vital that children are never seen as in any way responsible for their exploitation, nor should parents be blamed for exploitation of their children by others. In the past, children who were sexually exploited were often seen as "child prostitutes" (Hallett *et al*, 2017) and in this way seen as responsible for the abuse they were experiencing. Views on this have changed drastically and it is now clear that children should be seen as victims being exploited by abusive adults.

POSSIBLE SIGNS OF CHILD CRIMINAL OR SEXUAL EXPLOITATION

There are a range of potential warning signs that a child may be being exploited:

- Going missing from home or care
- Alcohol and drug use
- Physical injuries
- Offending
- Receipt of gifts/expensive items from unknown sources

- Poor mental health, self-harm or thoughts/attempts at suicide
- Angry and aggressive
- Travelling unexpectedly
- Estranged from family
- Absence from school
- Repeated sexually transmitted infections/pregnancies/terminations

Clearly some of these possible signs alone will not mean that a child is being exploited. It is very unlikely that a child will disclose exploitation because of fear of their perpetrators and limited self-efficacy. Practitioners increasingly use checklists or toolkits to assess risk and determine whether a child is being exploited. In England, there are numerous child sexual and criminal abuse protocols and risk assessments. However, it is important not to become overly reliant on checklists as they can miss some "less typical" victims, and professionals should utilise their own professional decision-making, rather than being solely guided by checklists.

If a child is found by the police after going missing, or found under the influence of alcohol or drugs, and there are suspicions of child exploitation, they will contact children's services. The police can remove the child to a safe place. If the child is considered at risk of harm, a child protection conference will be held. A child protection plan would be put in place, so that services can be provided to meet the needs of the child and family; it may be at this point that neglect is also identified. Many local authorities have multi-agency safeguarding hubs (MASH) to co-ordinate a response to child exploitation, and some have specific child exploitation teams. The multi-agency teams are likely to be made up of children's services, police, youth offending, mental health, drug and alcohol services, education, and there may be voluntary sector organisations specifically working with child sexual or criminal exploitation. There may also be a specialist parent support worker.

CONTEXTUAL SAFEGUARDING

Contextual safeguarding is a theory developed by Carlene Firmin (2020) which is considered in response to both child sexual and criminal exploitation. It is an approach to understanding and responding to young people's experiences of significant harm beyond their families, for example, sexual or criminal exploitation, which is often known as "extra-familial abuse". Contextual safeguarding recognises that relationships young people have in their neighbourhoods, schools and online can feature abuse and violence. Those young people experiencing neglect will likely be spending more time out of their homes and on the streets. Parents and carers can have little control or influence in these situations, and young people's experience of sexual and criminal exploitation will often have strategically further undermined carer–child relationships, deliberately isolating the child. Thus, professionals, carers, family members and community organisations can work together to both protect young people and to disrupt the organised activity of perpetrators/extra-familial abusers. This extends the work of child protection social workers and suggests the need to work with wider community partners to protect children in their localities (Firmin and Knowles, 2020). This can be described as the social model of child protection (Featherstone *et al*, 2020). Examples of contextual safeguarding initiatives include working in the community to create safer spaces for children to meet, where they cannot be targeted by would-be perpetrators.

CASE STUDY: DEAN

Dean is groomed by a street gang in his neighbourhood to traffic drugs across the country. He is approached by them when hanging out with his friends at a local takeaway food shop. The influence of those who have groomed him means that Dean does not come home when his parents ask him to, and he stops answering their calls whilst running drugs. Slowly, Dean's parents lose control over him, and when they try and lock him in the house, he physically attacks his mother to get out. Dean is one of six young people who have been approached at the takeaway shop for the purposes of drug trafficking. Within a contextual safeguarding model, the risk in Dean's neighborhood, and the group who have groomed him, appear to be more influential than his parents. In a traditional approach, it would be Dean and his family who would be referred, assessed and receive intervention to address his behaviour, often with little impact.

In the contextual safeguarding system, extra-familial settings and relationships could be subject to this process; so the takeaway shop, street gang and/or Dean's peer group may be referred into a safeguarding system, assessed, discussed by a partnership, and then subject to an intervention, as a means of keeping Dean safe. Strategically and operationally, the safeguarding partnership is made aware of the trend associated with the takeaway shop, the street gang, six young men, and the issue of drugs trafficking. They work together to design a plan for disrupting risk in that context, and therefore safeguard all six young people affected by it.

Assessing this issue may in turn address the challenges of neglect that Dean is facing at home, whereas intervening with Dean's family alone is unlikely to impact on the risks he is facing in the community. Thus he is facing risks from both angles.

(Taken and adapted from Wirral Safeguarding
(see link in resource list below))

PRACTICE WITH CHILDREN WHO ARE BEING OR HAVE BEEN EXPLOITED

Children who are neglected will be supervised less well by their carers and may be more accessible. Children who have also experienced neglect may also have poor attachment to their caregivers from early in their lives and find it difficult to trust people and make stable relationships later in life (see also Chapter 3). When children have been further exploited by perpetrators, the impact on them can be huge, having a damaging impact on mental and physical health, further compounding existing difficulties. Young people who have been subject to exploitation are likely to experience fear, feeling unsafe, shame, stress, guilt, and be unlikely to be able to trust others. Their understanding of relationships can be very distorted, making it difficult for them to form healthy relationships in the future. When working with children and young people who have been subject to neglect, their trauma can be further compounded by sexual and criminal exploitation, creating complex difficulties. There are a range of approaches that can be useful:

- individual therapeutic work;
- group-based therapeutic work;
- family counselling;
- youth work support;
- education, training and employment support;
- sexual health and relationship education;
- drug and alcohol support;
- supported placements.

However, there is limited evidence on the successes of strategies for working with exploitation, with only one large-scale quantitative evaluation of intervention outcomes specifically related to child sexual exploitation (Bovarnick et al, 2017).

There is a tendency for responses to exploitation, especially sexual exploitation, not to focus on perpetrators, but instead on how to remove the child from danger of exploitation, which can result in the child or young person being placed in secure accommodation (Jago, 2011). Secure accommodation or residential care can sometimes provide children with a sense of safety and security that they may not have felt elsewhere; however, it can also have significant drawbacks. When children are moved into residential care, it can leave them feeling that they are to blame for their own abuse because they are confined while their abusers are not; young people can feel as if they are being punished. Physical safety when not combined with positive relationships and therapeutic support is not ultimately effective in helping children and young people who have experienced exploitation (Hallett *et al*, 2017). In addition, physical safety may not be ensured in secure or residential care, in part because perpetrators target such accommodation, because they know that the young people who live there are vulnerable (Munro, 2011).

CASE STUDY: TEEGAN

"Teegan", a white British young woman, was sexually exploited from the age of 12. From the age of 13, Teegan was taken by a Turkish man to a variety of "parties" across England that she reports were in nice houses and in some cases described as "mansions". In these houses, Teegan would be raped by several men, from a range of ethnicities, who were paying to use her. Teegan described a book being available with photographs and ages of all of the girls being sexually exploited by this particular group. Men could choose which girls they wanted. Teegan reported men paying those who were exploiting her up to £500 for an hour with her. Groups of men could also request one girl to share between them over a night, where the rape of the girl would be filmed. The operation involved men working the streets to pick up vulnerable girls, forming "relationships" with them by grooming them and then passing them on to the men who controlled the business. If Teegan ever refused to comply, she would be beaten and her family threatened. Following the abuse, Teegan took several overdoses, was placed in secure accommodation, and self-harmed by cutting and ligaturing sometimes on a daily basis. Teegan described the abuse that she experienced as serious and organised, and is unwilling to make a formal complaint for fear of repercussions from those involved in the operation.

(Based on an interview with a young person. Taken from Local Government Association, 2014, available at: https://bit.ly/3iyytYN)

The most important aspect of practice in situations of cumulative neglect and exploitation is to provide supportive, consistent, durable relationships for children and young people (Fursland, 2017). Direct work with children and young people who are considered to be at very high risk of exploitation, or who have already been exploited, is found to be most effective. There has been significant success reported with specialist foster placements for extremely high-risk child sexual exploitation-experienced and/or trafficked young people in keeping children safe and supported (Hallett *et al*, 2017). Interventions are often assigned to specialist third sector organisations. A study undertaken by Hallett (2021), asking children what they valued in such circumstances, identified the need for a trusted and supportive adult/carer who can directly involve the young person in decision-making and help to give them a say. See the resource list at the end of this chapter for the Check your Thinking toolkit, and a resource pack for tackling exploitation.

Young people who have been exploited will have felt controlled and without a say for long periods of time, feeling silenced and afraid, potentially also having felt this throughout their childhood of neglect. Taking part in activities together and chatting whilst doing so is valued and experienced as less stressful by young people. Anything that strengthens feelings of agency and belonging, for example, developing interests and activities that will improve overall well-being and happiness, will be helpful (see Chapter 8). Children who have been exploited, criminally or sexually, may feel that the major focus of attempts to help has been on them as objects of surveillance, on their errant behaviour, focusing on deficits and wrongdoing, rather than on their strengths. Understanding what matters for the young person is an essential aspect of any approach, and keeping them in the loop about what is happening and about decision-making is also highly valued. Positive forward planning for education, employment and housing will also help young people to reframe their futures. Practitioners could also refer parents to Parents Against Child Exploitation (PACE), an organisation that supports parents whose children are at risk or have been sexually or criminally exploited, and to disrupt the exploitation.

Whilst much is done with third sector organisations, social workers in local authority children's teams do much good work with children who are being or have been exploited, as the following case study demonstrates.

CASE STUDY: SALLY

Sally lived with her mother Pauline and sister Sophie. Sally suffered a stroke at a young age and has a diagnosis of learning difficulties. She became known to children's services when she was 12 years old, when her mother realised her daughter was pregnant (the father being an adult male). Sally was placed on the child protection register when her pregnancy became evident. Sally gave birth at age 13 and her child has since been adopted. During her pregnancy, Sally was subsequently abused by another adult male. This case study describes the student social worker's involvement with Sally whilst her practice educator was working with Pauline.

There were several concerns relating to Sally and her circumstances. This included, firstly, the fact that she had engaged in sexual relationships with two adults and had become pregnant below the legal age of consent. Due to Sally's additional learning needs, there was a concern as to what extent she understood the concept of consensual sexual relationships. It seemed Sally had limited ability to safeguard herself from further potential sexual harm or abuse. The second concern was the fact that her mother, Pauline, had failed to notice her daughter was pregnant until extremely late into the pregnancy. This led to questions surrounding Pauline's parenting capacity and ability to safeguard Sally. The social worker worked alongside Pauline to help her prevent Sally being sexually exploited in the future. She also helped Pauline move her family to a new area away from the perpetrators, although they were not perceived to be part of a gang. Pauline was further supported to begin to implement boundaries for Sally around not spending long periods out of the home, or on the computer.

After Sally had given birth and her child had been adopted, she became very withdrawn. Prior to this, Sally enjoyed going out with her sister and mother and attending an animal sanctuary for volunteer work. She had also enjoyed school. Annie, the student social worker, began to work with Sally, with a focus on building trust, education about healthy relationships, and internet safety. It was vital to build rapport so that a positive working relationship could be developed. This was done through Annie adopting a relaxed and friendly manner right from the start, especially as the earlier focus had been on Sally's "negative" behaviour. It was apparent to Annie right away that Sally had a good sense of humour. During one early visit, Sally told Annie that she had annoyingly interrupted her as she was watching a classic TV series. Annie told Sally she used to watch the same programme when she was younger. Sally invited Annie to watch it with her, which they did together over a cup of tea.

Gradually building this trust was vital as Sally had previously been in situations where she had been taken advantage of and did not know who she could trust. Annie also focused on rebuilding Sally's positive social networks; together they visited the animal sanctuary. This in turn, helped to regain Sally's confidence, as she began to understand how to keep herself safe and build independence. She returned to school and the school reported she was catching up with her academic work.

(Annie Fligelstone, student social worker)

CONCLUSION

Children who are neglected or who have experienced neglect can be vulnerable, and may be particularly susceptible to exploitation; consequently, they are often targeted by those who wish to exploit them. These children often do not realise that they are being exploited, so it is important for parents and carers to look out for signs of exploitation. Relationships are key to building trust and helping children and young people recover from the multiple impacts of neglect and exploitation.

PRACTITIONER TIPS

- Look out for signs of exploitation.
- Work with others in the team around the child to remove the child from perpetrators.
- Work closely with the child to build trust.
- Develop a meaningful relationship with the child.
- Work with the child to build self-esteem.
- Focus on the child's strengths, not on deficits.
- Take an activity-based approach of doing things with the child, rather than concentrating only on report writing or preparing for meetings.
- Work to support the child's interests.

An independent inquiry was carried out into child sexual abuse between 2016–2021 (IICSA), which has published a series of reports making recommendations relating to abuse in a range of settings, including, for example, health care and custodial institutions (see link to resources below).

FURTHER READING AND RESOURCES

Websites

Check your Thinking – resource for working with child exploitation: https://www.checkyourthinking.org/

Contextual Safeguarding Research Programme website: https://www.contextualsafeguarding.org.uk

Parents Against Child Exploitation (PACE): https://paceuk.info/

Other resources

NSPCC (2021) *Protecting Children from Sexual Exploitation*, available at: https://learning.nspcc.org.uk/child-abuse-and-neglect/child-sexual-exploitation

Independent Inquiry into Child Sexual Abuse (IICSA) research reports, available at: https://www.iicsa.org.uk/reports-recommendations/publications/research

National Crime Agency (undated) *County Lines*, available at: https://bit.ly/3CX7nnw

Wirrall Safeguarding Children's Partnership (undated) *Case Study*, available at: https://bit.ly/3k1Af50

Local Government Association (2021) *Tackling Child Exploitation: Resources pack*, available at: https://bit.ly/3vUC9Hw

Maxwell N and Wallace C (2021) *Child Criminal Exploitation in Wales*, available at: https://bit.ly/3vW0f4q

Chapter 8

Approaches when working with children who have experienced neglect

INTRODUCTION

This chapter considers some of the things that children looked after value (many of whom have experienced neglect and abuse). It is important that each child is seen as an individual and responded to as such. Each child will value different things, and we need to understand "what matters" for every child. There is no one way to work with children who have suffered neglect, but certain underlying principles and approaches are helpful. In considering what children in care value, we draw on the Bright Spots study (2017–2022), findings from the Care Inquiry in England (2013) and the Care Review in Scotland (2018). The chapter then looks at some approaches that have been designed to support young people who have experienced abuse and neglect, including the Secure Base Model, social pedagogy, Human Givens approach, Video-Interactive Guidance, and ways to build resilience.

LANGUAGE

It is very important to consider the language we use when working with children in care. Language can be stigmatising and can unwittingly mark children out as different. The use of terms such as LAC has been experienced as particularly stigmatising by children, especially because of the implied *lack* in their status (Children's Commissioner for Wales, 2016). Acronyms generally are unhelpful and experienced as alienating, for example, CIN (child in need), which also has negative connotations, as does the phonetic implication of "sin" in that a child or young person has done something sinful or wicked. Similarly, children prefer not to be seen as being in a placement, but rather living at home or in a family (TACT, 2019). The term contact also conceptualises seeing family as something different from what other families do, whereas "spending time with family" normalises it and is more inclusive.

Siblings and peers are also terms that young people may find ostracising, preferring brothers and sisters, and friends, as preferable. Many professionals refer to "mum" when talking about a child's mother, for example, in a case conference; this can be seen as patronising. We should call her by her name, as is the case for everyone else in the meeting. Language is important and it is vital that we consider the impact of some of the terms we use.

REFLECTIVE EXERCISE

- Think about the language you use when working with children who have experienced neglect. Make a list of the terms and acronyms you use.

- Which terms and acronyms do you think might be unhelpful or even hurtful?

WHAT CHILDREN VALUE

Bright Spots

The Bright Spots Programme is a partnership between Coram Voice and the University of Oxford (Lewis and Selwyn, 2021). It supports local authorities to listen to their children in care and care leavers about the things that are important to them. The programme has three underlying principles:

- Focus on what children and young people say about their lives and what is important to them.

- Ensure that the views and experiences of children influence service development and strategic thinking.

- Share good practice between local authorities by encouraging opportunities for learning and development.

Since 2013, the Bright Spots study has surveyed almost 10,000 care-experienced young people, from over 50 local authorities in England and Wales, asking them about the things that are important to them. The surveys were co-produced with 170 young people and the questions are based on what the young people said was important to them. From the survey, the study developed "well-being indicators" (Coram Voice, 2020), suggesting four domains in particular that are important for children and that relate to the four Rs:

1. **Relationships**, including being able to see members of their birth family, having a trusted social worker, a close friend and living with adults whom they trust. Having a pet is also valued by young people.

2. **Resilience**, including enjoying school, being supported in school, access to a range of activities and hobbies, access to nature, and access to the internet – even more important during the Covid-19 lockdowns.

3. **Rights**, including having an accessible social worker, not being made to feel different, feeling safe and free from being bullied.

4. **Recovery**, understanding the reasons they came into care, being able to talk to the adults they live with about their feelings, happy with how they look and being able to share their worries.

A detailed diagram setting out these indicators can be found at: https://www.education.ox.ac.uk/research/bright-spots/.

The Bright Spots study, Care Inquiry and Independent Care Review worked with local authorities to help them consider how they might respond to these findings, and developed a range of initiatives as a result. Some examples include setting up a five-a-side football team to combat loneliness (important for children who have experienced neglect), and starting a dance class workshop to build self-esteem (similarly vital for children who have been made to feel unworthy or not valued). A Practice Bank of examples has been created (see list of resources at the end of the chapter).

REFLECTIVE EXERCISE

Looking at the well-being indicators above, it is helpful to think about the young people with whom you work and have experienced neglect.

- Do they have a good friend?

- Are they happy about how they look?

- Do they have hobbies?

These are just some aspects to discuss with children and work on together.

Care Inquiry

An inquiry into the care system was undertaken in 2013 (Boddy, 2013). Inquiry activities included consultation events with a range of people with direct experience of care or the work of the care system. The Inquiry also co-ordinated a review of the research evidence by an academic group, responded to queries and submissions, and used social media to encourage a wide interest in the issues.

The main conclusion from the Inquiry was that 'permanence' for children in care means 'security, stability, love and a strong sense of identity and belonging'. This was not connected to legal status, children did not need to be adopted to experience this, and one route to permanence was not seen as necessarily better than any other. The Inquiry gave a strong message that it is the relationships with people who care for and about children that are the golden threads running through children's lives, and the quality of those relationships should be the lens through which we both approach and evaluate all we do. It is only through the building of relationships that children can begin to learn trust in those around them, and a major focus in recent years has been the development of relationship-based practice (Ruch *et al*, 2010; Ruch *et al*, 2020).

The Independent Care Review Scotland undertook a similar process in 2018 involving 5,500 people, over half of whom were children and young people with experience of the care system. The Review published The Promise, and found that:

> ...above all else children want to be loved, and recovery from trauma is often built on a foundation of loving, caring relationships...that will involve fundamentally shifting the primary purpose of the whole of Scotland's "care system" from protecting against harm to protecting all safe, loving, respectful relationships.

The Bright Spots study, Care Inquiry and Independent Care Review came to similar conclusions that relationships are central to young people's well-being. For children who have experienced neglect, those trusting, nurturing relationships will not have been forthcoming, and they may have difficulty building relationships.

RELATIONSHIPS WITH SISTERS AND BROTHERS

When children can no longer live with birth parents, they are moved to live with kinship carers, foster carers or are placed in residential care, and are often separated from their brothers and sisters. Similarly, if children are adopted they are also often separated from other children in their birth family, and may not have knowledge of each other (Ryan and Walker, 2016). Many children who have been neglected are from large family groups, where parents find it difficult to meet the needs of numerous children (Rees *et al*, 2021a and b), and then are likely separated. The Bright Spots survey found that relationships with birth family, especially sisters and brothers, are very important to children. Relationships with sisters and brothers are often the longest lasting, closest and most meaningful of people's lives (Beckett, 2021), as they have the same or similar backgrounds and life experiences. Brothers and sisters can provide reciprocal support to each other throughout their lives, and workers need to try wherever possible to keep children together or at a minimum provide support to maintain their relationships. Caring for several children from the same family may require specialist foster carers, and more detailed organisation and planning by social workers. We know how important relationships are for looked after children, and this should be a major consideration for practitioners (Beckett, 2021).

RELATIONSHIPS WITH CHILDREN

Supervising social workers as well as foster carers and adopters all need to think about their relationships with children. It is vital that children are not overlooked when social workers are dealing with adults' needs. Social work has often been criticised for being process-driven, with recording of events taking precedence over building meaningful relationships with children. Diaz (2020), in a study of children, found that they were frustrated and sceptical of the review process as they did not have relationships with the adults involved, including the Independent Reviewing Officer. Building this rapport and trust with children who have experienced neglect is essential. The Talking and Listening to Children (TLC) Project produced resources for practitioners, foster carers and adopters to help them communicate better with children (see resources at the end of this chapter). These are often used with trainee social workers.

Having established the importance of relationships in children's lives, this chapter now focuses on a range of approaches designed to promote relationships, recovery and resilience.

LIFE STORY WORK

Children who have experienced neglect may have difficulty with issues of identity and self-worth. It is difficult to value yourself if others have not devoted time to you or cherished you. It may also be difficult to understand why birth parents were not able to care for you or meet your needs and why professionals made the decisions they did. Children separated from birth family are often denied the opportunity to know information about their families and the reasons they are no longer living together (Ryan and Walker, 2016). When children are in care and do not have access to birth family, it is difficult to find out the information required. Life story work might reduce the likelihood of children seeking knowledge or making contact with birth family through social media, if workers and carers are open and honest. Much information becomes lost or forgotten, and there are many examples of children who have been adopted not knowing whether they have brothers and sisters, what time they were born, or other details about their lives. Identity is based very much on your family of origin and place within it.

In these circumstances, family life story work can be helpful, but only if done well. A scoping review of life story work was undertaken by Hammond *et al* (2021) who found that whilst it had the potential to be extremely helpful to young people, this was only when completed within a trusting, co-productive working alliance, where there was a meaningful relationship with the worker helping to create the life story. The quality and detail of the life story work is vital, so that aspects are not missing or incomplete. Guides to help with undertaking life story work include that by Ryan and Walker (2016) and Hammond and Cooper (2017).

SECURE BASE MODEL

The Secure Base Model, developed by Schofield and Beek (2018), considers how we can work with a child who has been abused and neglected so they can grow in confidence and feel they belong. The model has five dimensions which form part of helping a child to feel secure and have a sense of belonging (2018, p. 270), as follows.

	Care-giving thinking	Care-giving behaviour	Child thinking	Child behaviour
AVAILABILITY **Helping child trust**	What does this child need? I need to keep the child in mind at all times.	Remains alert and available, encourages child to explore.	I matter. I am safe. I can return. I can trust.	Uses carer as a secure base when anxious.
SENSITIVITY **Helping child manage feelings**	I need to put myself in the shoes of the child.	Tunes into child. Helps child make sense of experience.	My feelings and behaviour make sense.	Reflects on feelings of self and others, is empathetic. Has coherent life narrative.

	Care-giving thinking	Care-giving behaviour	Child thinking	Child behaviour
ACCEPTANCE **Building child's self-esteem**	I take pleasure in the child. I trust in the child's potential for good.	Promotes positives and enables child to feel successful.	Other people have thoughts and feelings to be taken into account.	Approaches activities with confidence. Enjoys success.
CO-OPERATION **Helping child feel effective**	How can I help the child to feel more effective and competent?	Promotes autonomy, accepts defiance, sets boundaries.	I feel effective. My views are important. I can compromise.	Is appropriately self-reliant. Negotiates and co-operates.
FAMILY MEMBERSHIP **Helping the child to belong**	Family boundaries can be flexible. Children can be members of more than one family.	Helps child to belong to both families.	I have rights & responsibilities. Feel connected to more than one family.	Incorporates the foster/ adoptive family into public and personal identity.

(Taken from Schofield and Beek, 2018, p. 18)

The Secure Base Model helps a child begin to feel secure and develop trust in those around them, and also helps the child to feel more confident and begin to think of the needs of others. It is important to think about how to help a child develop a narrative about their lives and, as recommended in a trauma-based approach, understand their experiences of neglect. One of the domains is for children to experience small aspects of success and enjoy taking part in activities, which in turn promotes feelings of achievement in their agency; this is also discussed under resilience in Chapter 9.

REFLECTIVE EXERCISE

- How might you use the Secure Base Model with children whom you work with who have experienced neglect?

- Reflect on how you have helped a child to understand and have a sense of belonging to both their birth and foster/adoptive family.

SOCIAL PEDAGOGY

Social pedagogy offers a conceptual framework that provides rich possibilities for reflecting on the nature of the supportive relationship between carer and child.

(Boddy, 2011, p. 105)

Social pedagogy is a theoretical discipline for work with and through relationships. It has been defined as 'education in its broadest sense', where professional–child relationships are a significant component (Petrie *et al*, 2006, p. 2). It relates to viewing the individual as a whole person (body, mind and spirit) and fundamentally the relationship of the individual to others (Hart and Monteux, 2004). Through establishing connections to other people and to the community, children and young people develop their identity and meaning in life. Social pedagogy is concerned with the upbringing of children, that unifies all elements of living and learning to contribute to their everyday experiences and development (Petrie *et al*, 2006). Within foster and residential care, a social pedagogic approach can build on existing practice and enhance experiences for children and young people through improved trusting relationships (The Fostering Network, undated). Trust may be very difficult for children who have been neglected because they have not been able to trust that they will be provided for, nurtured or necessarily cared for.

Cameron (2013) notes that relationships can have a significant contribution to the outcomes for children in care, as it has been argued that even when all the right frameworks and structures are in place, it is the quality of relationships that will determine whether a child in care feels "cared about" on a day-to-day basis. This is especially important for a child who has experienced neglect, who will not have felt cared for or cared about. Thus, spending time with, coming alongside and listening to children is vital. Relationships can be both professional and personal at the same time; both are necessary but neither alone is sufficient (Boddy, 2011). For some children in care, good parenting, developing relationships, love and affection may not be enough (Rushton, 2013). Children who have been neglected may lack trust in those around them and be reluctant to build relationships with any new people in their lives. Therefore the need is for something over and above, often termed therapeutic parenting (Boddy, 2011) (see Chapter 9), or parenting supported by therapeutic approaches.

THE HUMAN GIVENS APPROACH

The Human Givens Approach (Griffin and Tyrell, 2013) suggests that all children and indeed people have biologically based psychological needs that must be met in order to maintain psychological health. These are nearly as important as those for food, protection, housing, and medical health. Maslow's (1954) Hierarchy of Needs highlights the vital importance of psychological needs that should be met for psychological well-being. The Human Givens Approach (Griffin and Tyrell, 2013) suggests that these needs are:

- security and safety;
- attention;
- connection with others;
- a sense of belonging and status;
- being psychologically stretched;
- a balance between autonomy and control;
- a sense of purpose and meaning, often to be found in relationships.

We can see how these domains closely correlate to child neglect, as, for example, when a child is not being given attention, this is both physical and psychological. The child may be upset by not receiving attention, or they may not be having their physical needs met as a result of lack of attention. Additionally, they may not be supervised and are therefore at risk of harm. Similarly, safety is physical, whereas security is a psychological concept relating to how secure a child feels. A child who has been neglected may not feel safe because they will be constantly worried that their needs may not be met. This hierarchy of needs is important to be aware of when working with children, especially in order to help recognise where there is an omission in meeting them.

VIDEO-INTERACTIVE GUIDANCE

Video-Interactive Guidance (VIG) is a way to work with birth parents, or for foster carers and adopters to help them become more attuned to their children (especially important for neglected children where caregivers were not attuned and have not responded to children's needs or given them nurturing attention). It focuses on strengths and helps parents and carers to improve their communication with children. VIG often works alongside other interventions, for example, parenting programmes.

The model is based on a set of values and beliefs:

- Everybody is doing the best they can at the time.

- All people, even in adverse circumstances, have the capacity for change.

- People have an innate desire to connect with others.

- People must be actively involved in their own change process.

- Affirmation and appreciation of strengths is key to supporting change.

- Recognition and empathetic regard for what people are managing, builds trust.

(Kennedy *et al*, 2017)

The model uses a trained guider (these have been psychologists, social workers or support staff) to work with the parent/carer via an appreciative, respectful relationship. The guider carefully sets up and records the parent/carer and child doing an activity, or playing together. The aim is to capture the best possible interaction available from the recording, as the model is premised on the notion that watching yourself perform a behaviour well increases feelings of self-efficacy (Maxwell and Rees, 2019). The film is edited into the most successful "micro-moments", to be watched back together. Parents/carers who witness their own positive interactions with their child will be prompted to repeat these behaviours, promoting attachments.

> *Findings have shown that VIG is associated with increases in parent understanding of their children, enhanced relationships and improved parenting strategies that led them to implement new approaches.*

(Maxwell and Rees, 2019, p. 1,417)

The micro-moment clips exemplify attuned attention, even where these are the exception to normal patterns of parenting. In the shared review, the guider supports the parent/carer to watch these micro-moments of film. The guider provides therapeutic insight as the parents'/carers' internalised perception of themselves is challenged (so they can see that not everything they do is wrong) leading to increased sensitivity, responsiveness and attunement towards the child (Balldin *et al*, 2016). The parent/carer then decides what they would like to work on in the following session. These sessions are repeated until attuned communication is achieved. Numerous studies have found VIG to improve attunement by parents, foster carers and adopters (NSPCC, 2015a; Kennedy *et al*, 2010; Kennedy *et al*, 2017; Maxwell and Rees, 2019). Research also suggests that children really enjoy VIG, and the strengths-based aspect of it. Children who have been neglected enjoy being the centre of the attention and being involved in the planning, recording, playing together and watching themselves back (Maxwell and Rees, 2019).

VIG is non-intrusive, non-judgemental and well received by parents and carers, many of whom learn new parenting strategies without being directed by workers (Maxwell and Rees, 2019; Maxwell *et al*, 2019). (Also see resources at the end of this chapter.)

The following case study demonstrates how workers use several approaches, in this case VIG and PACE, when working with a child who has been neglected.

CASE STUDY: KATIE

I worked with Katie and her dad Steve, completing three VIG cycles over four months. The success reflected a seamlessly joined parallel intervention, with me as VIG Guider and Jen, the family worker, working as a team in partnership with the family.

When we met, Steve's relationship with Katie was tense. He found himself constantly on alert, bracing himself for the next conflict. Katie had been diagnosed with Asperger's and they had struggled in their relationship for as long as he could recall. Katie was clearly desperate to connect with him, her distressed behaviours reflecting the emotional neglect she was living with every day. Steve described Katie's behaviours as angry and challenging, telling me, 'She just pushes against me and screams at me when I try to get her to do things, like getting dressed for school or going to bed'. Jen described Katie's sadness and low self-esteem, wanting to spend fun time with her dad but noting, 'He just shouts'.

For the first cycle, I filmed 10 minutes of Katie and Steve playing with a ball in the garden, which had turned into play-wrestling as Katie tried to dive for the ball before Steve did. When I micro-analysed the film to select clips and "stills" reflecting attuned interactions, I looked for moments of exception in Steve's attunement to Katie. I carefully selected a "still" of successful eye contact, and chose clips that showed Steve's smile and gentle tone of voice in response to Katie's verbal and non-verbal initiatives. None of the clips were more than three seconds long, this being ample for VIG micro-analysis in a shared review. In the final clip, he was astonished to see Katie supporting his shoulder to prevent him rolling on the ball and hurting himself. The camera had captured the care in her eyes in that moment as she reached behind him to push the ball away, and the way he had moved towards her in response to her hand on his shoulder. He realised that they did have a connection after all.

Jen had recently been working with Steve on some specific areas of his parenting through a PACE (Playfulness, Acceptance, Curiosity, Empathy) course, that linked well with the themes emerging from this first shared review. She had been encouraging him to plan in "special time" for play every day, but she sensed that his hopelessness and low self-confidence was sapping his motivation to persevere. However, the clips and "stills" had given Steve irrefutable proof of their connection. Steve became increasingly attuned to Katie, and my final film captured long periods of attuned interaction, with the dance-like quality we VIG Guiders love to see.

As the work drew to a close, and Steve was ready for VIG to end, we all reflected on the change that had happened. Steve and Katie's relationship was flourishing, with Katie's behaviours reflecting her increasing emotional well-being. She smiled and laughed more, showed greater independence, took pride in her achievements, was more settled in school, and clearly loved her dad's attentions. Steve said he hardly ever shouted any more, that his confidence had grown and that he was finally enjoying being a dad.

(CarolAnn Stirling, VIG Guider and social worker)

THE TEAM AROUND THE CHILD

Although not much has been written about the team around the child, working together with other professionals is essential for children who have been neglected (see Chapter 5). It is important that all members of the team around the child are invited to meetings, including school staff and foster carers. Education staff and foster carers spend most time with children and are likely to know the child best, and it is important that they are listened to. Fostering Wellbeing is a project in Wales (2022) that provides joint training of foster carers, social workers, education and health staff in aspects of therapeutic approaches and parenting, so all of those working with the child are taking the same approach. As a result of the joint training, foster carers have reported being included in the team around the child, have become more confident to advocate on the child's behalf and feel more valued by the rest of the team. If carers are listened to and respected, they will be better able to support the child. The role of the foster carer "pioneer" is also being developed within the Fostering Wellbeing project to help support foster carers, to share information and resources and highlight the vital significance of the foster carer role.

CONCLUSION

In this chapter, we have covered a range of approaches and underpinning principles to working with children who have experienced neglect. All of these involve building relationships, increasing trust, nurturing, and bolstering the child's self-esteem. Many of these approaches include practical steps that can be taken forward together in practice. The supervising social worker should be bringing all members of the team around the child together so people can work collaboratively. It is vital that all members of the team around the child are listened to and valued equally.

PRACTITIONER TIPS

- Be thoughtful about the language you use when talking about or to children in care.

- Relationships are key to helping children.

- Think about the four Rs – relationships, resilience, rights, and recovery.

- The team around the child need to communicate regularly.

- The team around the child should work in complementary ways.

- Several approaches can be utilised at the same time and work successfully together.

FURTHER READING AND RESOURCES

Websites

Bright Spots Programme: https://bit.ly/3Xo35uX

Short VIG animation, available at: https://edpsy.org.uk/blog/2018/vig-an-animation/

Other resources

Coram Voice (2020) *The Voices of Children in Care and Care Leavers on What Makes Life Good*, available at: https://bit.ly/3W6Htly

Coram Voice (2021) *Having Fun and Combatting Loneliness*, available at: https://bit.ly/3GZuWfo

Sheen M (2022) *I Broke Down Hearing Kids' Care Stories*, available at: https://bbc.in/3QzkRZP

Chapter 9

Therapeutic parenting: skills for working with children who have experienced neglect

INTRODUCTION

This chapter addresses what practitioners, foster carers and adopters may need to consider when supporting children who have experienced neglect. The chapter considers some of the skills of therapeutic parenting that can help children who have experienced neglect begin to regain trust and confidence.

PARENTING AND THERAPEUTIC PARENTING

All children need love and stability in order to thrive, and for children in care this is provided by the corporate parent:

A strong corporate parenting ethos means that everyone from the Chief Executive down to front-line staff, as well as elected council members, are concerned about those children and care leavers as if they were their own. This is evidenced by an embedded culture where council officers do all that is reasonably possible to ensure the council is the best "parent" it can be to the child or young person.

(DfE, 2018, p. 6)

Thus, in principle, a looked after child who has been neglected should be able to have the same expectations of nurture, protection, support and care from their corporate parent, as any other child might expect of a reasonable parent.

There is a clear need for skilled practitioners and carers when working with children who have experienced neglect:

How we respond to and protect children from the harmful effects of neglect is one of the most pressing and challenging aspects of safeguarding work in this country.

(Brandon *et al*, 2020, p. 58)

It is known that children in care are more likely than the general population to suffer from mental health problems (Meltzer *et al*, 2003), to have physical and learning disabilities, special educational needs, and emotional and behavioural difficulties (DfE, 2018; May-Chahal and Palmer, 2018). The harm that children have suffered in the past via neglect affects both their behaviour and expectations. It is therefore vital to ensure that those people who will be caring for children – whether that is parents, kin, foster carers, social workers or adopters – have the necessary understandings and capabilities (Pithouse and Rees, 2014; Brandon *et al*, 2020). For children who have experienced neglect, caring by foster carers and adopters frequently extends beyond normative experiences of parenting (Murray *et al*, 2011, p. 149); this is often known as therapeutic parenting. Responding to neglect requires skilled and thoughtful practitioners; if such practitioners are not available, children can continue to be subject to trauma and neglect, even when in public care (see Chapter 6).

DYADIC DEVELOPMENTAL PSYCHOTHERAPY

Dyadic developmental psychotherapy (DDP) provides a framework for supporting looked after and adopted children to recover from trauma, through parenting support (Golding, 2014, p. 19). Based on theories of attachment, DDP helps support parents and carers to manage challenging behaviour, whilst also remaining connected with the child. DDP requires extensive training (levels 1–3); level 1 is useful for practitioners, but training all staff to level 3 would be very resource-intensive.

DDP was developed by Dan Hughes, who realised the vital role that foster carers, adopters and residential workers play as attachment figures for children who have experienced neglect, abuse, trauma and loss, and who find it hard to trust adults. He found that ordinary parenting failed to support children sufficiently and thus developed a therapeutic approach. This is achieved based on the principles of PACE (playfulness, acceptance, curiosity and empathy). There is a DDP Network of resources to support parents, carers and practitioners (see resources list at the end of this chapter).

PACE

The PACE principles of parenting provide helpful guidance on how to interact therapeutically with looked after children, particularly those who have experienced neglect and trauma. PACE is developed from an attachment-based model (Golding and Hughes, 2012), which looks at where children may become anxious, hyper-vigilant (sensitive) and feel unloved and unlovable (as covered in Chapter 3).

PACE is an acronym for:

- Playfulness

- Acceptance

- Curiosity

- Empathy

The PACE approach was developed by Dan Hughes, a US clinical psychologist who specialises in working with young people who have experienced abuse and neglect. All children need love, but this is not always enough; some children will be helped by a more therapeutic approach. PACE was developed to help a child feel safe and begin to trust people. As already highlighted, this is essential for children who have been neglected and have not been able to trust in those who care for them.

Playfulness

This is about creating an atmosphere of interest and light-heartedness when communicating with a child, using a playful and light voice tone, akin to story-telling, rather than using an authoritative or irritated tone. Playfulness is about fun, a sense of joy and spontaneity. This implies the strength of relationship between worker or carer and child, rather than letting any irritation emerge. Workers and carers should not take themselves too seriously and be able to laugh at their mistakes. The primary goal is to enjoy being together, without any specific goals.

This is a particular difficulty for professionals, particularly social workers, who can be process-driven and have reviews to complete. In an evaluation of Fostering Wellbeing (Rees, 2019), only one child remembered any social worker positively, and this was a worker who had taken her out for a meal without wanting to fill out forms; this made the child feel far more valued. Children who have been neglected will be keenly aware that their needs are not being addressed and that the social worker has an agenda of their own. Social workers should consider the impact on children of being so process-driven.

Acceptance

Unconditional acceptance is at the core of every child's sense of security and safety. It is vital to listen to and accept the child's emotions and feelings, but not any unwanted behaviour. For true acceptance to take place, it is important that the parent, worker or carer has a routine of seeing the child beyond any difficult behaviour. Expressing difficult emotions about themselves or others (e.g. 'I don't have any friends', 'No one likes me', 'I'm awful') should be listened to and not be challenged. Part of this approach is to accept and acknowledge all feelings, using empathy and curiosity.

Curiosity

It is important to be curious about the child's thoughts, feelings, wishes and intentions. Curiosity is also important for discipline to be effective. If a child behaves inappropriately, ask what they are feeling. Curiosity involves a quiet, accepting tone that conveys a simple desire to understand the child, for example, 'What do you think was going on?', 'What do you think that was about?' or 'I wonder what...?'

Empathy

Empathy lets the child feel your compassion. Being empathic means actively showing the child that their inner life is important to you and that you want to be with the child in hard times. Understanding and expressing your own feelings about the child's experience can often be more effective than praise. For example, if a child says, 'You don't care', you can respond by saying, 'That must be really hard for you. I feel sad that you experience me as not caring', rather than denying this and causing conflict.

(Taken from www.ddpnetwork.org)

REFLECTIVE EXERCISE

Think about how many children you have worked with recently where you have focused on completing information for an assessment. Do you think the children were aware of this?

Managing challenging situations

PACE, like social pedagogy, focuses on the whole child. It helps children be more secure with their parents, workers or carers. Children begin to feel safer, more accepted and more able to trust those who care for them. Using PACE can reduce the level of conflict, defensiveness and withdrawal that tends to be ever present in the lives of children who have experienced abuse and neglect. Using PACE enables the worker/ carer to see the strengths and positives in the child, beyond any negative behaviour (Hughes, 2019). Using PACE is a long-term commitment, a culture and ethos of parenting that is ongoing and not a short-term practice.

ENDORSEMENT OF PACE

The carers I have worked with therapeutically, following the principles of PACE, have been more trusting and open in communicating with me, and I have developed a better understanding of how best to support them and the children in their care as a result. I have found that carers are more likely to be Playful, Accepting, Curious and Empathetic towards the children in their care, if I adopt the same approaches when working with them.

When children display challenging and difficult to manage behaviours, this can be stressful for foster carers and can lead to placements ending. I have experienced several occasions when therapeutic parenting has helped in these circumstances to repair the relationship between the carer and child. I have supported foster carers to empathise with the child again, which in my experience is commonly what carers find difficult when managing ongoing challenging behaviour, especially if it is directed towards them. Using a therapeutic parenting approach can prevent placements breaking down, and result in a more settled and secure relationship between the child and carer in the long term.

(Olivia Clark, social worker)

CASE STUDY: PETER

Peter is aged seven. He lives with his grandmother, who is his special guardian. His mother lives in the family home intermittently, tending to come and go without warning. She takes no role in parenting Peter. At school, where he is in Year 3, Peter finds it very difficult to let adults be in charge. He often takes control of situations, telling the other children when it is time for break or lunch, and being "bossy" when playing. He is sometimes very affectionate towards his class teacher, often finding reasons to chat or call to her. At other times, he can express a lot of anger towards her, shutting himself in the toilet and telling her he hates her.

Peter's grandmother and teacher identify that Peter behaves similarly towards them both. They wonder whether Peter might feel that he is unloveable and expect adults to behave in a very unpredictable way. They agree that the world must feel quite scary for Peter. Together they make a plan to show Peter that he can trust adults to be reliable and caring, and that he himself is loveable. They both use PACE with Peter, being playful, accepting, curious and empathetic. The school's special educational needs co-ordinator (SENCO) identifies a key worker in school who can build a strong relationship with Peter, with regular one-to-one time built into his timetable. When Peter has a bad day, the class teacher takes the time to acknowledge the difficult day, letting him know that she still likes him and wants him in her class. School staff supervise Peter's peer interactions more closely, and help him practise waiting for his turn, and letting other children make decisions about games.

The headteacher arranges an after-school training session on attachment and trauma for all school staff. All the adults who have contact with Peter in school agree on a script to use when Peter shows controlling behaviour: 'We know it can be scary to let grown-ups be in charge. In our school, the children can trust the grown-ups to keep them safe.' Peter's grandmother seeks advice from the adoption support service about how to set boundaries with Peter's mother so that she cannot come and go from the family home without warning.

(Taken from DfE and PAC-UK, undated, available at: https://bit.ly/3vVFc2b)

Many children who have been neglected respond well to sensitive, responsive parenting, but some will not. However, it is important that the practitioner does not always assume the problem lies with the child, and to demonstrate curiosity when a child is not progressing. Children may be unhappy in their home even if it is stable and nurturing. It is therefore vital that we see children by themselves and take time to listen to them; failure to listen to children's concerns and respond to their unhappiness might constitute further neglect. Expressions of unhappiness by children might include, for example, deliberate actions intended to lead to placement breakdown, self-harm, running away, or making allegations about carers (Sinclair *et al*, 2004; The Fostering Network, 2022). However, practitioners should not make assumptions that a child's unhappiness stems from previous experiences of neglect but should always approach the situation with professional curiosity: this is when professionals question and challenge the information they receive, identify concerns and make connections to enable a greater understanding of a young person's situation. Much of this is about practitioners having knowledge and an ongoing relationship with children to understand what is concerning them. Diaz's study of Independent Reviewing Officers who had little or no ongoing relationship with children between reviews found that their work could not be participatory and became process-driven (Diaz, 2020). Getting to know children and meaningfully gleaning their views is vital for all those working with children.

Practitioners must be able to ask awkward questions and suspect the worst is possible. Most importantly, carers and practitioners must encourage the child to talk, give them time, and listen to what they say. The relationships that children have with carers and practitioners are vital, and as the Independent Care Review in Scotland found, it is important to maintain safe, loving, respectful relationships (2018).

QUALITIES OF CARERS

Those who are assessing carers should look for carers who:

- have a strong support network;
- have an ability to manage diversity and celebrate the uniqueness of each child;
- can provide stability and commitment in relationships;
- can resolve conflict;
- are open and co-operate;
- take a child-centred approach.

(Beesley, 2011, p. 107)

Attention should also focus on family culture and values, consideration of who else lives in the home, any other children placed in the family, and the impact of birth children and extended family.

It is vital that carers and their families are able to be open, warm, sensitive, and to express their own emotions. Children who have been neglected will have difficulty in developing and maintaining trusting relationships. This means that they may find it difficult to make attachments to people, as in the past, their needs were not responded to. The importance of attachment theory is discussed in Chapter 3. Thus, children and young people will need carers to treat them with unconditional positive regard wherever possible.

Foster carers will have their own attachment styles, depending on their childhood history. A carer who has strong, close and positive relationships is more likely to be able to attune and sensitively respond to children's needs. Attunement describes how sensitised a person is to a child's emotional needs and moods. Someone who is well attuned is able to respond to a child with appropriate language and behaviours, based on the child's emotional state. They will have an awareness of their own feelings and try not to let these impact on the interactions. Obviously, this is not always possible, but self-awareness is key.

Practitioners and foster carers need to be able to reflect on their own lives and backgrounds, and their own childhood experiences. Being able to reflect on your own life and being aware of your emotional state and what you bring to a relationship is known as emotional intelligence, and this is an important skill for both carers and practitioners. At its heart, emotional intelligence (Howe, 2008) is the ability to read, understand and respond effectively to your own and other people's emotions.

Both foster carers and practitioners must be able to demonstrate authentic and emotional warmth and be attuned to the needs of the child. Cameron and Maginn (2008), when discussing corporate parenting, note seven pillars of parenting:

- primary care and protection;

- helping the child to foster a secure attachment;

- helping the child to feel positive about themselves;

- helping the child become more emotionally competent;

- encouraging the child to develop self-management skills;

- helping the child to develop resilience;

- helping the child to develop a sense of belonging.

Cameron and Maginn (2009, p. 22) note that parenting is more than providing physical necessities for a child:

> Parenting involves more than those activities that ensure a child's survival..."caring for" is not the same as "caring about" and while the former can mean providing the physical necessities of life, like safety, food, clothes, warmth and somewhere to sleep, the process of "caring about" demands a subtle form of parental involvement that includes availability, thoughtfulness, responsibility, guidance and emotional investment.

This distinction between "caring for" and "caring about" is helpful for practitioners to consider. The following short exercise may help you to think more carefully about the difference between each.

REFLECTIVE EXERCISE

List four behaviours and actions where you, as a social worker, social care worker or foster carer, demonstrate that you are caring for and caring about children.

- Caring for

- Caring about

Foster carers play an essential role in caring for and about children, yet they are often left out of decision making and the team around the child (Rees *et al*, 2019; The Fostering Network, 2021; Rees and Handley, 2022). This may be because other professionals do not always value their expertise. Yet foster carers often have the closest relationship with children in care and, because they spend so much time with children, are likely to understand their daily difficulties, trials and tribulations. They are therefore often best placed to advocate on their behalf (Rees, 2019). It is helpful for foster carers to learn about and develop therapeutic parenting skills.

Naish's book (2018), *The A-Z of Therapeutic Parenting*, is a useful resource for social workers, foster carers and adopters, covering a range of principles and techniques, highlighting the importance of establishing strong and clear boundaries. The book covers a wide range of presenting difficulties, including, for example, sleep issues, social media and how to help children negotiate transitions.

KEY ASPECTS OF CARING

We now consider some of the key aspects of caring by parents, foster carers and adopters, starting with the often-overlooked aspect of touch.

Touch

Children in public care are no different from other children; they also need ongoing positive, helpful touch for normal brain development. It is a fundamental human need and necessary for healthy social, emotional, cognitive and physical development. Children who have been neglected will often have not been nurtured or physically comforted by their caregivers. This may make it difficult for a child to understand physical reassurance, or be afraid of it. The absence of human touch for a neglected child will impact on their emotional sense of self, and yet children in care routinely exist in a "no-touch" vacuum (Rees, 2019).

Sadly, as any psychologist would confirm, it is likely that [children] would view the absence of touch as their fault, leaving them feeling "untouchable" and even more devastating for a child, they may think of themselves as unlovable.

(Maginn, 2020, p. 1)

In his book, *My Name is Why*, Lemn Sissay talks about his experiences of being a child in care and the lack of touch for children. He has also recorded a talk about lack of touch, entitled 'When all you need is a hug: personal experiences of the UK care system', where he discusses the emotional damage of not being touched or hugged as a 12-year-old boy in a children's home (see resource list at end of chapter). Both the book and recording are very accessible practice resources to help workers understand what it feels like (from a child's perspective) not to be touched by those who supposedly "care" for and about you.

Parents naturally touch their children on a daily basis. Touch is fundamental to all child development; it is part of human relationships, for bonding, demonstrating affect, empathy and as a means of offering comfort to a child. Some children in care who have been neglected may have received little in the way of affirmatory touch. If they have also been physically or sexually abused, this will heighten their anxiety. When children have experienced abuse, this often makes professionals and carers cautious, in case children might experience touch as threatening, or that touch, even well-meaning, may lead to allegations (Sinclair *et al*, 2004; The Fostering Network, 2022). Whilst it is important to establish boundaries and the right to privacy for young people, the absence of touch for children in care is extremely unnatural and damaging, particularly if it is not forthcoming from those in a caring and parenting role. This was exacerbated for some young people during the Covid-19 pandemic where they had little contact with the outside world (Roberts *et al*, 2021). The lack of physical reassurance from foster carers could also pose a safeguarding issue. Maginn (2020, p. 1) has produced a table of positive and harmful touch:

A quick guide to touch

Helpful touch	Harmful touch	Absent touch
Supportive or reassuring	Hitting or hurting	The absence, or withholding, of touch, impairs the child's emotional development
Offering comfort	Overfamiliar or sexual	
Shows acceptance and approval	Controlling or restraining	
Light stroking touch can reduce cortisol levels in people who are depressed	Rough handling	Professional anxiety surrounding touch deprives children of a basic human need
	Can trigger the fight, flight or freeze response	
Touch can help an upset child to be calm and regulated	Causes an increase in the level of cortisol	Withholding touch can confuse: the child would not understand why they are "untouchable"
A hug can be used to celebrate success	Can lead to impulsive, irrational, defensive behaviour	

(Taken from Maginn, 2020, p. 1)

Maginn concludes that there is a 'need for protection from adults in the parenting role who opt for the clinical soul-destroying absence of touch' (2020, p. 1).

Views from foster carers and children

Rees (2019), writing about a study of foster care, noted the lack of positive touch for children in care and how detrimental this is. In the study, one carer mentioned how some children who had been neglected do not even understand the purpose of touch, and gave an example of a young person who had asked 'Why do people hug each other?' (Rees, 2019, p. 90). Another carer discussed how children gradually became accustomed to positive touch, as trust in the foster family developed:

Suzie was never like that, but now I often give her a cwtch (Welsh for cuddle). I tug her hair a little bit, playful you know, and she loves it. (Stella).

(Rees, 2019, p. 90)

In the same study, young people also talked about the positive impact of touch and how it helped them to settle into foster families, and gave some helpful examples of how natural, responsive touch was experienced as reassuring and affirming (Rees, 2019, p. 89):

'He [foster carer Josh] is a very funny person and a serious person as well. I found living with him he'd mess about [saying] 'Do you want a fight?', just messing around. We got on so well from the moment I came here. He is very hands on, he'd put his arms round me and stuff. From

both Hazel [female carer] and Josh...with Hazel embracing...it would be when I needed it, whereas with Josh it would often be a friendly arm around. With Hazel it would be a motherly hug.

(Callum, aged 16, living in foster care)

It is important that carers provide thoughtful, physical reassurance and comfort to young people in their care and consider the implications for children of living in a no-touch family zone.

Food

Food is another often overlooked aspect of caring for looked after children (Rees, 2019). Children who have been neglected will often have had negative experiences with food, by not having been provided with regular or sufficient food by their birth parents. This will make them feel anxious about where their next meal is coming from or want to hoard food to ensure they have a plentiful supply. Survival or hoarding behaviours can include:

- eating quickly, or consuming large quantities of food;
- hiding/hoarding food into their room/bags/pockets;
- not eating at family mealtimes but preference for eating alone;
- becoming upset if someone eats off their plate or being unable to share communal food;
- becoming upset if food is taken away;
- eating only familiar and "safe" foods.

When a child moves into a new foster home, it will be important that the foster carer is thoughtful and flexible about food, and that they are willing to respond to and accommodate the child's preferences and food choices. Whilst some may see children's food preferences as being picky or a fad, Brannon et al (1994) refer to this as children's "food personae", those choices and preferences specific to the child. Rees (2019, p. 95) notes how young people who had experienced neglect talked to her about how their experiences of lack of food impacted their behaviour, and how the foster carers' approach and being provided with plentiful amounts was well received:

I used to have to eat very quickly because if I didn't there would be hands in, nicking bits of food because there were so many [children] of us living in one house. We grew accustomed to each other and so we used to fight for food and stuff because there was never enough sausage and chips and stuff. Now I don't have to fight for food, but I still eat very, very quickly. Now I've never had it so easy, I get twice as much, and I don't have to fight for it!'

(Callum, aged 16, living in foster care)

A foster carer told us about how they respond to children's food experiences and "personae", and how it was helpful to involve children in the choosing and preparation of food.

CASE STUDY: ADAM

Adam, aged 14, has arrived at his foster home. He is very thin and very quiet, dishevelled and withdrawn. Adam is completely compliant and follows all instructions. The social worker accompanying Adam says he has been brought into care for neglect.

After a few days you notice food is missing from cupboards or the fruit bowl. You are providing Adam with three to four meals a day, which includes one school meal. Adam is said to be a "fussy eater". He is also able to access the "treat box", which includes small bars of chocolate, some sweets, biscuits and crisps. Adam is told he can have two to three treats a day.

On entering his room to change bedlinen, you notice a smell – you find rotting fruit untouched under the bed and 15 treats, all untouched.

Things you can do as a foster carer:

- Remove any rotten items and replace with fresh. You may wish to do this for a few weeks until Adam settles into your home.

- Suggest to Adam that now he has settled in, would he like a treat box for his room. Ask what he may like in it. Limit the item number to, say, five to six treats. If he fills the box more, these should be non-perishable.

- Go shopping with Adam to buy things for his treat box.

- Ask him to date-check his treat box items, so out of date items can be replaced.

- Plan meals with him.

- Go shopping together for the ingredients.

- Get him to help prepare and make meals, especially ones he likes, then ones he's tried and liked with foster carers.

- Check meals are sufficiently filling.

If this does not slowly change Adam's relationship with food, intervention with professionals may be needed. Sometimes work with foster carers is needed to help them understand why youngsters do this and how else they can support the child. Time and patience are a must.

Social workers must realise that there is not always a quick fix, and that it can and does take years for a child/young person to believe food is readily available and it is their right to have it. Sometimes there is no fix, and this behaviour continues into adulthood. Other food issues – bulimia, starving themselves and/or both, will need extra professional support to both carer and child/young person.

(Lindsay Warren, foster carer, South Wales)

For more information on food issues in looked after children, see Vaughan and Burnell, 2021.

RESILIENCE

Children who feel they are to blame for the losses and hurts in their life will often experience any hurt as evidence of this, confirming their beliefs (Cairns and Cairns, 2016). Memories of previous trauma can also be triggers for strong emotions (see Chapter 6). However, children can also pick up on even the smallest of hints and clues that they are loved and valuable, and this can help them to begin to transform their beliefs about themselves. Taking a strengths-based approach (Saleeby, 1996) with children who have been neglected is important as they may be unaware of any qualities and skills they have, with much focus of work with children having been deficit-based. Many have written about resilience and Gilligan, in particular, has written about increasing resilience when working with children in care (2001; 2007). As noted in Chapter 6, our understanding of ACEs and trauma-informed work has increased in recent years, and helping a child to increase their self-esteem and agency can bolster their resilience, their ability to feel more confident, and their ability to face hurdles and setbacks in life. Gilligan (2001) simply defined resilience as comprising a set of qualities that helps a person to withstand many of the negative effects of adversity. The approach of workers and carers (see Secure Base Model, Chapter 8) can help a child begin to feel more loved and loveable. Helping a child access wider family networks (birth or foster family), community resources and activities can create a wider framework of support (Pithouse and Rees, 2014).

Factors that help build resilience include:

- a secure attachment to caregivers;
- a sense of self-esteem and self-efficacy;
- sociability;
- relationships with other supportive adults;

- supportive friendship networks;

- regular attendance and continuity of schooling;

- opportunities for problem-solving;

- opportunities to develop hobbies and talents.

(Taken from Beesley, 2011, p. 119)

It is helpful to remember the African proverb that 'It takes a village to raise a child' when trying to identify what local community organisations a child can be linked in to. Looking at what a child is interested in and trying out any number of extra-curricular activities provides opportunities for the child to find something they may be good at, however obscure. Each new activity creates a repertoire of experiences on which the child can draw, talk about and remember, and can even be useful for future curriculum vitae. Helping children to experience "success" can inculcate aspiration and ambition. Organisations have communities of members who are also interested in the same hobby or activity, and this widens the pool of possible supportive relationships for the child. Children enjoy doing activities with workers or carers, because it is easier to talk when not sitting face-to-face, across a desk (Ferguson, 2008). Also, doing an activity together allows the worker or carer to model that it is good to explore and take a risk in trying something, and possibly fail. This might be a very simple approach but one which many young people have benefitted from.

In a study of fostering by Rees (2019), foster carers gave examples of how they tried to build resilience:

> We have always said that whatever child comes, our focus is around what makes them tick. And you do. You will find something...there will be something. So we throw ourselves into different activities all of the time. Something clicks, which is rather wonderful for us.

(Ian, foster carer)

> I find whatever teenager I had with me, it doesn't matter what their home problem was, whatever their problem...every single teenager had something, a brilliant artist, a brilliant dancer or maybe a fantastic cook. Or they were fantastic at doing their makeup or whatever...Everybody had something good, and I found that within them...and that was magical to me and I tried to find it in all of them and once I found what it was, we worked on it.

(Cilla, foster carer)

Here, we can see how making efforts to try different activities, hobbies and interests might help a child to find things that they are good at which may in turn extend their connections within the community, and begin to improve their self-esteem.

Lastly, spending time outdoors and in nature has long been seen as beneficial for health and well-being, especially for children. Gordon (2019) created a case study with nine foster carers (looking after 18 children) who undertook a 'Fostering Outdoor Play' course to encourage and support child-led, outdoor play (see Play Wales in the resources list at the end of the chapter). The post-training questionnaires identified that children and young people were spending 33 per cent more time outdoors during weekends, with reported improved well-being, and some of the families had begun new activities, including scootering, river and woodland play (Gordon, 2019).

CONCLUSION

This chapter has considered therapeutic parenting and the need for skilled and committed caregivers. The chapter covered some aspects of therapeutic parenting, including dyadic developmental psychotherapy and PACE. We conclude by highlighting the importance of some of the seemingly basic, yet essential and often overlooked aspects of care for children who have experienced neglect and the many ways in which self-esteem and resilience can be bolstered. It is important to recognise that with the right support, children who have experienced neglect can become productive and even more loving than their peers (Furnivall and Grant, 2014).

PRACTITIONER TIPS

- Take time to listen to children.
- Try to become emotionally attuned to children.
- Foster carers should gradually try to provide and build up physical reassurance to children.
- Explore children's preferences for food.
- Go shopping for food together with children.
- Begin to cook together with children.
- Explore extra-curricular activities and enjoy trying new challenges together.

FURTHER READING AND RESOURCES

Play Wales: https://www.playwales.org.uk/eng/nature

Sissay L (undated) *When All You Need is a Hug: Personal experiences of the UK care system*, available at: https://www.youtube.com/watch?v=B88dCHJ9Rvg

Talking and Listening to Children Project resources: https:// talkingandlisteningtochildren.co.uk

Conclusion

As outlined in the introduction to this book, this practice guide intends to offer an applied text for busy professionals who are supporting children in a range of settings. Neglect, as a form of child maltreatment, is conceptually complex and often results from a range of causes, meaning that there are no simple, prescriptive solutions for practice. What this book therefore offers is clear and accessible guidance by drawing on examples of what others have found to work well in a variety of situations. This book has emphasised the importance of ensuring we intervene in circumstances where children are living with neglect as early as possible, whilst also making sure we ask ourselves if we are providing the most appropriate type of support to meet the child's needs.

The early chapters of the book focused on the conceptualisation of neglect and the importance of reflecting on our individual assumptions, values and experiences of parenting or caring for children, and of being parented in childhood. These chapters encouraged practitioners to pause and consider what assumptions underpin their professional judgements in relation to those children living with neglect and in need of support and protection. The third and fourth chapters explored the impact of neglect and the challenges of recognising and assessing neglect. The fifth chapter drew attention to the importance of interprofessional collaboration, foregrounding the persistent challenges of working effectively with others when responding to the intricacies of neglect, across organisational and professional boundaries at individual, cultural and structural levels.

The second half of the book focused on approaches to working with children who have experienced neglect. We considered adverse childhood experiences (ACEs), and related to this, trauma-informed approaches when working with children and developing tailored responses to their needs. The seventh chapter covered child exploitation and possible approaches to working with this, including contextual safeguarding and a societal response, highlighting the importance of the relationship between children and practitioners. The final two chapters presented the needs of children who have experienced neglect and some of the things they value. Chapter 8 included a range of conceptual lenses through which to approach sensitive and reflective work with children. The final and ninth chapter covered therapeutic parenting and the need for attuned and thoughtful practitioners: some of the often forgotten, yet life enhancing elements of parenting are covered, including food and touch. Lastly, we covered resilience and building children's self-esteem, skills and aspirations.

The role of the corporate parent cannot be underestimated, with the aim that everyone in the team around the child and across the local authority treat children in care as if they were their own, having the same level of expectation and ambition for them. We highlight that children are not a homogeneous group but have their own individual experiences, needs and interests that need to be understood and channelled. We advise against a process-driven approach when working with children, but rather encourage taking the time to get to know each child and cherish their individual qualities. Children will be keenly aware of your agenda to complete paperwork; this depersonalises and undervalues the individual child.

The golden thread throughout this book is the importance of the relationships we build with children, and the quality of those relationships should be the lens through which we both approach and evaluate all we do. Children need to feel loved, and we should help preserve all friendships and loving, respectful relationships in their lives. Children can recover from the negative experiences and challenges they have faced to become strong, empathetic, caring and productive members of society. Value your role in helping young people to flourish and find their path in life, and enjoy the privilege of being able to do so.

References

Action for Children (2010) *Neglecting the Issue: Impact, causes and response to child neglect in the UK*, Stirling: University of Stirling

Ainsworth M and Bell S (1970) 'Attachment, exploration and separation: illustrated by the behaviour of one-year-olds in a strange situation', *Child Development*, 41, pp.49–67

Allnock D (2016) 'Child neglect: the research landscape', in Gardiner R (ed) *Tackling Child Neglect: Research, policy and evidence-based practice*, London: Jessica Kingsley Publishers, pp. 101–129

Baginksky M (2008) *Safeguarding Children and Schools*, London: Jessica Kingsley Publishers

Balldin S, Fisher P and Wirtberg I (2016) 'Video feedback intervention with children: a systematic review', *Research on Social Work Practice*, 28:6, pp. 682–695

BASW (2019) *Anti-Poverty Practice Guide for Social Work*, Birmingham: BASW, available at: https://bit.ly/3XeJ3Dp

Beesley P (2011) *Ten Top Tips for Identifying Neglect*, London: BAAF

Beckett S (2021) *Beyond Together or Apart: Planning for, assessing and placing sibling groups*, London: CoramBAAF

Bellis MA, Ashton K and Hughes K (2016) *Adverse Childhood Experiences and their Impact on Health-Harming Behaviours in the Welsh Adult Population*, Cardiff: Public Health Wales/Liverpool, Centre for Public Health, Liverpool John Moores University

Berridge D, Sebba J, Cartwright J and Staples E (2021) 'School experiences of children in need: learning and support', *British Educational Research Journal*, 47:6, pp. 1,700–1,716

Boddy J (2011) 'The supportive relationship in public care; the relevance of social pedagogy', in Cameron C and Moss P (eds) *Social Pedagogy and Working with Children and Young People*, London: Jessica Kingsley Publishers, pp. 105–124

Boddy J (2013) *Understanding Permanence for Looked After Children*, Brighton: University of Sussex, available at: https://bit.ly/3H4R1tj

Bovarnick S, Scott S and Pearce J (2017) *Direct Work with Sexually Exploited or at Risk Children and Young People: A rapid evidence assessment*, available at: https://uobrep.openrepository.com/handle/10547/623177

Bowlby J (1969) 'Attachment and loss', *The American Journal of Psychiatry*, 97, pp. 1,158–1,174

Brandon M, Bailey S, Belderson P and Larsson B (2013) *Systematic Review of Neglect in Serious Case Reviews in England*, London: NSPCC, available at: https://learning.nspcc.org.uk/research-resources/2013/neglect-serious-case-reviews

Brandon M, Belderson P, Warren C, Howe D, Gardner R, Dodsworth J and Black J (2008) *Analysing Child Deaths and Serious Injury through Abuse and Neglect: What can we learn? A biennial analysis of Serious Case Reviews 2003–2005*, Nottingham: DCSF

Brandon M, Sidebotham P, Belderson P, Cleaver H, Dickens J, Garstang J, Harris J, Sorensen P and Wate R (2020) *Complexity* and Challenge: A triennial analysis of SCRs 2014–2017, London: DfE, available at: https://bit.ly/3ZLRJmD

Brayden R, Atlemeier WI, Tucker D, Dietrich M and Vietze P (1992) 'Antecedents of child neglect in the first two years of life', Journal of Paediatrics, 120:3, pp.416–429

Brannon J, Dodd K, Oakley A and Storey P (1994) Young People, Health and Family Life, Buckingham: Open University Press

Bullock L, Stanyon M, Glaser D and Chou S (2019) 'Identifying and responding to child neglect: exploring the professional experiences of primary school teachers and family support workers', Child Abuse Review, 28, pp. 209–224

Bywaters P, Bunting L, Davidson G, Hanratty J, Mason W, McCartan C and Steils N (2016) The Relationships between Poverty, Child Abuse & Neglect: An evidence review, York: Coventry University and Joseph Rowntree Foundation

Cairns K and Cairns B (2016) Attachment, Trauma and Resilience: Therapeutic caring for children, London: CoramBAAF

Cameron C (2013) 'Cross-national understandings of the purpose of professional–child relationships: towards a social pedagogical approach', International Journal of Social Pedagogy, 2, pp. 3–16

Cameron RJ and Maginn C (2008) 'The authentic dimension of professional childcare', British Journal of Social Work, 38:6, pp. 1,151–1,172

Cameron RJ and Maginn C (2009) Achieving Positive Outcomes for Children in Care, London: Sage

Care Quality Commission (2018) Growing Up Neglected: a multi-agency response to older children, Manchester: Ofsted, available at: https://bit.ly/2KNXgFf

Carter V and Myers MR (2007) 'Exploring the risks of substantiated physical neglect related to poverty and parental characteristics: a national sample', Children and Youth Services Review, 29:1, pp. 110–121

Child Safeguarding Practice Review Panel (2020) Executive Summary: Annual report 2020, available at: https://bit.ly/3mWhim1

Children's Commissioner for Wales (2016) The Right Care: Children's rights in residential care in Wales, Swansea: Commissioner's Office, available at: https://bit.ly/3W9iA93

Coordinated Action Against Domestic Abuse (CAADA) (2014) In Plain Sight: The evidence of children exposed to domestic violence, available at: https://bit.ly/3QB6dRR

Crittenden PM (1992) 'Children's strategies for coping with adverse home environments: an interpretation using attachment theory', Child Abuse and Neglect, 316:3, pp. 329–34

Crouch E, Jones J, Stromplois M and Merrick M (2020) 'Examining the association between ACEs, childhood poverty and neglect, and physical and mental health: data from two state samples', Children and Youth Services Review, 116

Dalzell R and Sawyer E (2016) Putting Analysis into Child and Family Assessment (3rd edn), London: National Children's Bureau

Daniel B and Taylor J (2006) 'Gender and child neglect: theory, research and policy', Critical Social Policy, 26:2, pp. 426–439

Daniel B, Taylor J, Scott J, Derbyshire D and Neilson D (2011) Recognising and Helping the Neglected Child: Evidence-based practice for assessment and intervention, London: Jessica Kingsley Publishers

Daniel B, Burgess C, Whitfield E, Derbyshire D and Taylor J (2014) 'Noticing and helping neglected children: messages from Action on Neglect', *Child Abuse Review*, 23:4, pp. 274–285

Davie CE, Hutt SJ, Vincent E and Mason M (1984) *The Young Child at Home*, Windsor. NFER-Nelson

Davies C and Ward H (2012) *Safeguarding Children across Services*, London: Jessica Kingsley Publishers

De Bellis MD (2005) 'The psychobiology of neglect', *Child Maltreatment*, 10:2, pp. 150–172

DeCandia C and Guarino K (2015) 'Trauma-informed care; an ecological response', *Journal of Child and Youth Care Work*, 25, pp. 7–32

DePanfilis D (2006) *Child Neglect: A guide for prevention, assessment and intervention*, Washington DC: Department of Health and Human Services, Administration for Children, Youth and Families, Children's Bureau, Office on Child Abuse and Neglect

Department for Education (2014) *Court Orders and Pre-Proceedings for Local Authorities*, London: DfE

Department for Education (2017) *Child Exploitation: Definition and a guide for practitioners, local leaders and decision makers working to protect children from child sexual exploitation*, London: DfE

Department for Education (2018) *Foster Care in England*, London: DfE, available at: https://core.ac.uk/reader/151185950

Department for Education (2019) *Applying Corporate Parenting Principles to Looked After Children and Care Leavers: Statutory guidance for local authorities*, London: DfE

Department for Education and PAC-UK (undated) *Case Studies*, available at: https://bit.ly/3vVFc2b

Department of Health (2000) *The Framework for Assessment of Children in Need and their Families*, London: DH

Department of Health (2005) *Obesity among Children under 11*, London: DH

Department of Health (2017) *Co-Operating to Safeguard Children and Young People in Northern Ireland*, Belfast: DH

Devaney J and McConville P (2016) 'Childhood neglect: the Northern Ireland experience', *Research, Policy and Planning*, 32:1, pp.53–63

Diaz C (2020) *Decision Making in Child and Family Social Work: Perspective on child's participation*, Bristol: Policy Press

Dickens J (2007) 'Child neglect and the law: catapults, thresholds and delay', *Child Abuse Review*, 16:2, pp. 77–92

Doyle C and Timms C (2014) *Child Neglect and Emotional Abuse: Understanding, assessment and response*, London: Sage

Durkan M, Field F, Lamb N and Loughton T (2015) *1001 Critical Days: The importance of conception to age 2 period: a cross party manifesto*, available at http://www.1001criticaldays.co.uk/1001days_Nov15.pdf

English DJ, Thompson R, Graham JC and Briggs EC (2005) 'Toward a definition of neglect in young children', *Child Maltreatment*, 10:2, pp. 190–206

Erikson MF, Egeland B and Pianta R (1989) 'The effects of maltreatment on the development of young children', in Cicchetti D and Carlson V (eds) *Child Maltreatment*, New York, NY: Cambridge University Press, pp. 647–684

Erterm IO, Bingoler BE, Ertem M, Uysal Z and Gozdasoglu S (2002) 'Medical neglect of a child: challenges for paediatricians in developing countries', *Child Abuse & Neglect*, 26:8, pp. 751–761

Farmer E and Lutman E (2012) *Effective Working with Neglected Children and their Families: Linking interventions to long term outcomes*, London: Jessica Kingsley Publishers

Featherstone B, Firmin C, Gupta A, Morris K and Wroe L (2020) *The Social Model and Contextual Safeguarding: Key messages for practice*, available at: https://uobrep.openrepository.com/handle/10547/624925

Featherstone B, Gupta A, Morris K and White S (2018) *Protecting Children: A social model*, Bristol: Policy Press

Featherstone B, Morris K, Daniel B, Bywaters P, Brady G, Butning L, Mason W and Mirza N (2019) 'Poverty, inequality, child abuse and neglect: changing the conversation across the UK in child protection?', *Children and Youth Services Review*, 97, pp.127–133

Ferguson H (2008) 'Liquid social worker: rethinking welfare interventions as mobile practices', *British Journal of Social Work*, 38, pp. 561–579

Ferguson H (2016) 'Making home visits: creativity and the embodied practices of home visiting in social work and child protection, *Qualitative Social Work*, 17:1, pp. 65–80

Firmin C and Knowles R (2020) *The Legal and Policy Framework for Contextual Safeguarding Approaches*, available at: https://bit.ly/3XsBSHE

Furnivall J and Grant E (2014) *Trauma Sensitive Practice with Children in Care*, Insight 27, Glasgow: IRISS, available at: https://bit.ly/3GZ1czn

Fursland E (2017) *Caring for a Child Who Has Been Sexually Exploited*, London: CoramBAAF

Gardner R (2008) *Developing an Effective Response to Neglect and Emotional Harm to Children*, Norwich: UEA/NSPCC

Gilligan R (2001) *Promoting Resilience: A resource guide for working with children in the care system*, London: BAAF

Gilligan R (2007) 'Adversity, resilience and the educational progress of young people in public care', *Emotional and Behavioural Difficulties*, 12:2, pp. 135–145

Glaser D (2000) 'Child abuse and neglect and the brain – a review', *Journal of Child Psychology and Psychiatry*, 41:1, pp. 97–116

Golding KS (2014) 'The development of DDP-informed parenting groups for parents and carers of children looked after or adopted from care', *Adoption & Fostering*, 43:4, pp. 400–412

Golding KS and Hughes DA (2012) *Creating Loving Attachments: Parenting with PACE to nurture confidence and security in the troubled child*, London: Jessica Kingsley Publishers

Gordon H (2019) 'The natural environment and its benefits for children and young people looked after', in Mannay D, Rees A and Roberts L (eds) *Children and Young People 'Looked After'? Education, intervention and the everyday culture of care in Wales*, Cardiff: University of Wales Press, pp. 99–112

Gorin S (2004) *Understanding what Children Say: Children's experiences of domestic violence, parental substance misuse, and parental mental health issues*, London: National Children's Bureau

Gorin S (2016) 'Learning from children and young people about neglect', in Gardiner R (ed) *Tackling Child Neglect: Research, policy and evidence based practice*, London: Jessica Kingsley Publishers

Griffin J and Tyrell I (2013) *Human Givens: The new approach to emotional health and clear thinking*, Chalvington: Human Givens Publishing

Hallett S (2021) Check Your Thinking toolkit website, available at: www.checkyourthinking.org

Hallett S, Crowley A, Deerfield K, Staples E and Rees A (2017) *Review of the Wales Safeguarding Children and Young People from Sexual Exploitation (CSE) statutory guidance*, available at: https://bit.ly/3Gvn7wG

Hammond S and Cooper N (2017) *Digital Life Story Work: Using technology to help young people make sense of their lives*, London: BAAF

Hammond S, Young J and Duddy C (2021) 'Life story work for children and young people with care experience; a scoping review', *Developmental Child Welfare*, 2:1, pp. 213–315

Harford S (2018) *Child Neglect: How are schools addressing the issue?*, available at: https://bit.ly/2NJENfy

Hart N and Monteux A (2004) 'An Introduction to Camphill Communities and the BA in Curative Education', *Scottish Journal of Residential Child Care* 3, pp. 67–74

Haynes A (2015) *Realising the Potential: Tackling child neglect in universal services*, London: NSPCC

Hildyard K and Wolfe D (2002) 'Child neglect: development issues and outcomes', *Child Abuse & Neglect*, 26:6, pp. 679–695

HM Government (2018) *Working Together to Safeguard Children*, available at https://bit.ly/3QubyKR

HM Government (2020) *Keeping Children Safe in Education: Statutory guidance for schools and colleges*, available at: https://bit.ly/3CGJaPW

Hobbs CJ and Wynne JM (2002) 'Neglect of neglect', *Current Paediatrics*, 12:12, pp. 144–150

Holland S, Crowley A and Noakes L (2013) *An Investigation into Current Responses to Child Neglect in Wales*, Action for Children, NSPCC Cymru and Welsh Government/ Cardiff University

Home Office (2018) *Serious Violence Strategy*, available at: https://www.gov.uk/government/publications/serious-violence-strategy

Horwath J (2002) 'Maintaining a focus on the child', *Child Abuse Review*, 11, pp.195–13

Horwath J (2007) *Child Neglect: Identification and assessment*, Basingstoke: Palgrave MacMillan

Horwath J (2013) *Child Neglect: Planning and intervention*, Basingstoke: Palgrave MacMillan

Horwath J (2017) 'The missing assessment domain: personal, professional and organizational factors influencing professional judgement when identifying and referring child neglect', *British Journal of Social Work*, 37, pp. 1,285–1,303

Horwath J and Bishop B (2001) *Child Neglect: Is my view your view? Working with cases of child neglect in the North Eastern Health Board (NEHB)*, Dunshaughlin: North Eastern Health Board and University of Sheffield, available at: http://lenus.ie/hse/bitstream/10147/128258/1/Childneglect.pdf

Howe D (2000) *Attachment and Human Development*, Oxon: Taylor and Francis

Howe D (2005) *Child Abuse and Neglect: Attachment, development and intervention*, Basingstoke: Palgrave Macmillan

Howe D (2008) *The Emotionally Intelligent Social Worker*, London: Bloomsbury

Howe D, Dooley T and Hinings D (2000) 'Assessment and decision-making in a case of neglect and abuse using an attachment perspective', *Child and Family Social Work*, 5:2, pp. 143–155

Hughes D (2019) *Healing Relational Trauma through Dyadic Developmental Psychotherapy: An introduction to DDP*, available at: https://ddpnetwork.org/about-ddp/meant-pace/

Hunt J (2021) *Practising in Kinship Care*, London: Kinship, available at: https://kinship.org.uk/for-professionals/resources/kinshipcare_research/

Independent Care Review Scotland (2018) *The Promise*, available at: https://www.carereview.scot/wp-content/uploads/2020/02/The-Promise.pdf

Independent Inquiry into Child Sexual Abuse (2022) *The Report of the Independent Inquiry into Child Sexual Abuse*, available at: https://www.iicsa.org.uk/final-report.html

ISP Fostering (2021) *How Trauma impacts a Child's Brain*, available at: https://ispfostering.org.uk/childhood-trauma-brain-development/

Jack G and Gill O (2003) *The Missing Side of the Triangle: Assessing the importance of family and environmental factors in the lives of children*, Ilford: Barnardo's

Jago S (2011) *What's going on to Safeguard Children and Young People from Sexual Exploitation? How local partnerships respond to child sexual exploitation*, available at: https://bit.ly/3kdfzr2

Jobe A and Gorin S (2013) 'If kids don't feel safe they don't do anything – young people's views on seeking and receiving help from children's social care services in England', *Child and Family Social Work*, 18:4, pp. 429–438

Kempenaar M (2015) *Adoption Support Plans: Exploring the processes*, unpublished PhD thesis, Cardiff: University of Cardiff

Kennedy H, Landor M and Todd L (2010) 'Video Interaction Guidance as a method to promote secure attachment', *Educational & Child Psychology*, 27:3, pp. 59–72

Kennedy H, Ball K and Barlow J (2017) 'How does Video Interaction Guidance contribute to infant and parental mental health and well-being?', *Journal of Child Psychology and Psychiatry*, 22: 3, pp. 500–517

Kennedy M and Wonnacott J (2005) *Neglect of Disabled Children in Child Neglect: Practice issues for health and social care*, London: Jessica Kingsley Publishers

Kerr M, Black M and Krishnakumar A (2000) 'Failure to thrive, maltreatment and the behaviour and development of six-year-old children from low income, urban families; a cumulative risk model', *Child Abuse & Neglect*, 24:5, pp. 587–598

Levenson J (2017) 'Trauma-informed social work', *Social Work Practice*, 62:2, pp. 105–113

Lewis S and Selwyn J (2021) *An Evaluation of the Bright Spots Programme*, London: Rees Centre and Coram Voice, available at: https://bit.ly/3QAHrRU

MacAlister J (2022) *The Independent Review of Children's Social Care*, available at: https://childrenssocialcare.independent-review.uk/

Maginn C (2020) *A Modest Proposal to Help Looked After Children*, available at: https://bit.ly/3CKQGJu

Mannay D, Evans R, Staples E, Hallett S, Roberts L, Rees A and Andrews D (2017) 'The consequences of being labelled "looked after": exploring the educational experiences of looked-after children and young people in Wales', *British Educational Research Journal*, 43:4, pp. 683–699

Masson JM, Dickens J, Garside LBL, Bader KF and Young J (2019) *Child Protection in Court: Outcomes for children: establishing outcomes of care proceedings for children before and after care proceedings reform*, Bristol: University of Bristol

Maslow AH (1954) *Personality and Motivation*, London: Harper and Row

Maxwell N and Rees A (2019) 'Video Interaction Guidance: a return to traditional values and relationship-based practice?', *British Journal of Social Work*, 49:6, pp. 1,415–1,433

Maxwell N, Rees A and Williams A (2019) *Evaluation of the Video Interaction Guidance Service, Cornwall Council: Project report*, Cardiff: CASCADE, available at: https://bit.ly/3X6DoPV

May-Chahal C and Palmer C (2018) *Rapid Evidence Assessment: Characteristics and vulnerabilities of victims of online-facilitated child sexual abuse and exploitation*, London: Independent Inquiry into Child Sexual Abuse, available at: https://bit.ly/3Fqeqnv

McKeganey N, Barnard M and McIntosh J (2002) 'Paying the price for their parents' addiction: meeting the needs of the children of drug-using parents', *Drugs: Education, Prevention and Policy*, 9:3, pp. 233–246

McLeod A (2007) 'Whose agenda? Issues of power and relationship when listening to looked-after young people', *Child & Family Social Work*, 12:3, pp. 278–286

Meltzer H, Gatwood R Corbin T, Goodman R and Ford T (2003) *The Mental Health of Young People Looked After by Local Authorities in England*, London: Stationary Office

Monk C, Georgieff MK and Osterholm EA (2013) 'Research review: maternal prenatal distress and poor nutrition – mutually influencing risk factors affecting infant neurocognitive development', *Journal of Child Psychology and Psychiatry*, 54:2, pp. 115–130

Moran P (2009) *Neglect: Research Evidence to Inform Practice*, London: Action for Children, available at: https://bit.ly/3Tf6paZ

Morris K, Mason W, Bywaters P, Featherstone B, Daniel B, Brady G, Bunting L, Hooper J, Mirza N, Scourfield J and Webb C (2018) 'Social work, poverty, and child welfare interventions', *Child & Family Social Work*, 23:3, pp.364–372

Munro E (2011) *Munro Review of Child Protection: Final report – a child-centred system*, available at: https://bit.ly/3iuvPU6

Murray L, Tarren-Sweeney M and France K (2011) 'Foster carer perceptions of support and training in the context of high burden of care', *Child & Family Social Work*, 16:2, pp. 149–158

Naish S (2018) *The A-Z of Therapeutic Parenting: Strategies and solutions*, London: Jessica Kingsley Publishers

National Centre for Injury Prevention and Control (2019) *Preventing Adverse Childhood Experiences: Leveraging the best available evidence*, Atlanta, GA: National Centre for Injury Prevention and Control, available at: https://www.cdc.gov/violenceprevention/pdf/preventingACES.pdf

NHS Highland (2018) *Annual Report of the Director of Public Health 2018, Adverse Childhood Experiences, Resilience and Trauma-Informed Care: A public health approach to understanding and responding to adversity*, available at: https://bit.ly/eIJ4AzJ

NSPCC (2015a) *Spotlight on Preventing Child Neglect*, London: NSPCC

NSPCC (2015b) *Neglect: Learning from case reviews*, available at: https://bit.ly/3k8kb1t

NSPCC (2020) *How Safe are our Children? An overview of data on abuse of adolescents*, available at: https://bit.ly/3vYmffi

NSPCC (2021a) *Child Neglect: Statistics briefing*, available at: https://bit.ly/3kbaakf

NSPCC (2021b) *How do Childhood Experiences affect Brain Development?*, available at: https://bit.ly/3lI27Fx

NSPCC (2021c) *Statistics Briefing: Looked after children*, available at: https://bit.ly/2JcFWti

NSPCC (2021d) *Protecting Children from Sexual Exploitation*, available at: https://learning.nspcc.org.uk/child-abuse-and-neglect/child-sexual-exploitation

NSPCC (2022a) *Why Children Reveal Abuse*, available at: https://bit.ly/3GCIZGj

NSPCC (2022b) *Case Review Processes in UK Nations*, available at: https://bit.ly/3k07m9m

Ofsted (2009) *Learning Lessons from Serious Case Reviews*, London: Ofsted

Palmer C, Coffey A and Rees A (2023) *Adoption & Fostering*, forthcoming

Petrie P, Boddy J, Cameron C, Wigfall V and Simon A (2006) *Working with Children in Care: European perspectives*, Buckingham: Open University Press

Pithouse A and Crowley A (2016) 'Tackling child neglect: key developments in Wales', *Research, Policy and Planning: The Journal of the Social Services Research Group*, (Special Issue on Child Neglect), 31:1, pp. 25–37

Pithouse P and Rees A (2014) *Creating Stable Placements*, London: Jessica Kingsley Publishers

Pollack SD, Cicchetti D, Hornung K and Reed A (2000) 'Recognising emotion in faces: developmental effects of child abuse and neglect', *Developmental Psychology*, 36:5, pp. 1140–1145

Polonko KA (2006) 'Exploring assumptions about child neglect in relation to the broader field of maltreatment', *Journal of Health and Human Services*, 29:3, pp. 260–84

Public Law Working Group (2021) *Best Practice Guidance: Section 20 and section 76 accommodation*, available at: https://bit.ly/3Wa7PDb

Radford L, Corral S, Bradley C, Fisher H, Bassett C, Howat N and Collishaw S (2011) *Child Abuse and Neglect in the UK Today*, London: NSPCC, available at: https://bit.ly/3yIfjnY

Rees A (2019) 'The daily lived experience of foster care', in Mannay D, Rees A and Roberts L (eds) *Children and Young People "Looked After"? Education, intervention and the everyday culture of care in Wales*, Cardiff: University of Wales Press, pp. 85–99

Rees A, Maxwell N, Grey J, Corliss C, Barton A, Khan A, O'Donnell C and Silverwood V (2019) *Final Report for Evaluation of Fostering Wellbeing Programme 2019*, available at: https://orca.cardiff.ac.uk/id/eprint/128577/

Rees A, Dehaghani R, Slater T, Swann R and Robinson A (2021a) 'Findings from a thematic multi-disciplinary analysis of child practice reviews in Wales', *Child Abuse Review*, 30:2, pp. 141–154

Rees A, Fatemi-Dehaghani R, Slater T, Swann R and Robinson A (2021b) 'Findings from a thematic multi-disciplinary analysis of child practice reviews in Wales', *Child Abuse Review*, 30:2, pp. 141–154

Rees A and Handley B (2022) *Final Report: Evaluation of fostering wellbeing*, available from: https://orca.cardiff.ac.uk/id/eprint/154327/

Rees G, Stein M, Hicks L and Gorin S (2011) *Adolescent Neglect: Research, policy and practice*, London: Jessica Kingsley Publishers

Roberts L, Rees A, Mannay D, Bayfield H, Corliss C, Diaz C and Vaughan R (2021) 'Corporate parenting in a pandemic: considering the delivery and receipt of support to care leavers in Wales during Covid-19', *Children & Youth Services Review*, 128, 106155

Ruch G, Turney D and Ward A (2010) *Relationship-Based Social Work: Getting to the heart of practice*, London: Jessica Kingsley Publishers

Ruch G, Winter K, Morrison F, Hadfield M, Hallett S and Cree V (2020) 'From communication to co-operation: reconceptualising social workers' engagement with children', *Children & Family Social Work*, 25:2, pp. 430–438

Rushton A (2013) 'Enhancing adoptive parenting', in Tarren-Sweeney M and Vetere A (eds) *Mental Health for Vulnerable Children and Young People who are or Have Been in Foster Care*, London: Routledge, pp. 134–170

Ryan T and Walker R (2016) *Life Story Work: Why, what, how and when*, London: CoramBAAF

Safeguarding Board for Northern Ireland (2018) *Regional Core Child Protection Policies and Procedures for Northern Ireland*, Belfast: Safeguarding Board for Northern Ireland

Saleeby D (1996) 'The strengths perspective in social work practice extensions and cautions', *Social Work*, 41:3, pp. 296–305

Scannapieco M and Connell-Carrick K (2005) 'Focus on the first years: correlates of substantiation of child maltreatment for families with children 0–4', *Children and Youth Services Review*, 27:12, pp. 1,307–1,323

Schofield G and Beek M (2014) *Promoting Attachment and Resilience: A guide for foster carers and adopters on using the Secure Base model*, London: BAAF

Schofield G and Beek M (2018) *The Attachment Handbook for Foster Care and Adoption*, (2nd edn), London: CoramBAAF

Schore AN (2002) 'Dysregulation of the right brain: a fundamental mechanism of traumatic attachment and the psychopathogenesis of posttraumatic stress disorder', *Australian and New Zealand Journal of Psychiatry*, 36:1, pp. 9–30

SCIE (2016a) *Incomplete Information Sharing by Schools in Child Protection Conferences*, available at: https://bit.ly/3IEoSKN

SCIE (2016b) *Unfocused Discussion in Child Protection Conferences*, available at: https://bit.ly/3GAgOb9

SCIE (2016c) *Reluctance to Share Information in Front of Families in Child Protection Conferences*, available at: https://bit.ly/3ivhFC5

Scottish Government (2021) *National Child Protection Guidance for Scotland*, Edinburgh: Scottish Government

Scourfield J (2000) 'The rediscovery of child neglect', *The Sociological Review*, 48:3, pp. 365–382

Selwyn J, Meakings S and Wijedesa D (2015) *Beyond the Adoption Order: Challenges, interventions and adoption disruption*, London: BAAF

Shanahan ME, Runyan DK, Martin SL and Kotch JB (2017) 'The within poverty differences in the occurrence of physical neglect', *Children and Youth Services Review*, 75:1, pp. 1–6

Sharley V (2018) *Identifying and Responding to Child Neglect in Schools,* PhD thesis, Cardiff: Cardiff University

Sharley V (2019) 'Identifying and responding to child neglect in schools: differing perspectives and implications for inter-agency practice', *Child Indicators Research*

(Special Issue on Child Neglect), 13, pp. 551–571

Sharley V (2020) *The Critical Role of Schools in Protecting Vulnerable Children: Why schools and social workers need immediate support to respond to the effects of lockdown*, blog, Bristol: PolicyBristol, available at: https://bit.ly/3Qx4Pj6

Sheen M (2022) *Lifting the Lid on the Care System*, available at: https://bit.ly/3QwR7Np

Sidebotham P, Brandon M, Bailey S, Belderson P, Dodsworth J, Garstang J, Harrison E, Retzer A and Sorensen P (2016) *Pathways to Harm, Pathways to Protection: A triennial analysis of serious case reviews 2011 to 2014, final report*, London: DfE, available at: https://bit.ly/31i7e7u

Sinclair I, Gibbs I and Wilson K (2004) *Foster Carers: Why they stay and why they leave*, London: Jessica Kingsley Publishers

Sissay L (2022) 'Every one of us has a different story: a historic portrait of care system success', *The Guardian*, available at: https://bit.ly/3GZHXG3

Smith E, Johnson R, Andersson T, Belton E, Kyriacou S and Hodson D (2019) 'Evaluating the Graded Care Profile 2: comparisons with the original tool and factors affecting uptake and use of the updated tool', *Child Abuse Review*, 28, pp. 299–309

Sobsey D and Doe T (1991) 'Patterns of sexual abuse and assault', *Sexuality and Disability*, 9:3, pp. 243–259

Social Work England (2019) *Professional Standards*, available at: https://www.socialworkengland.org.uk/standards/professional-standards/

Spencer N and Baldwin N (2005) 'Economic, cultural and social contexts of neglect', in Taylor D and Daniel B (eds) *Child Neglect: Practice issues for health and social care*, London: Jessica Kingsley Publishers, pp. 26–42

Stevenson O (2005) 'Working together in cases of neglect: key issues', in Taylor J and Daniel B (eds) *Child Neglect: Practice issues for health and social care*, London: Jessica Kingsley Publishers, pp. 97–112

Stowman S and Donohue B (2005) 'Assessing child neglect: a review of standardised measures', *Aggression and Violent Behaviour*, 10:4, pp. 491–512

Suleman M, Sonthalia S, Webb C, Tinson A, Kane M, Bunbury S, Finch D and Bibby J (2021) *Unequal Pandemic, Fairer Recovery: The Covid-19 impact inquiry report*, London: The Health Foundation, available at: https://bit.ly/3W7sN5E

Sullivan PM and Knutson JF (2000) 'Maltreatment and disabilities: a population-based epidemiological study', *Child Abuse & Neglect*, 24:10, pp. 1,257–1,273

TACT (2019) *Language that Cares: Changing the way professionals talk about children in care*, available at: https://bit.ly/2SJ0D0d

Talge NM, Neal C and Glover V (2007) 'Antenatal maternal stress and long-term effects on child neurodevelopment: how and why?', *Journal of Child Psychology & Psychiatry*, 48:3/4, pp. 245–261

Taussig H, Dmitrieva J, Garrido E, Cooley J and Crites E (2021) 'Fostering healthy futures preventive intervention for children in foster care: long-term delinquency outcomes from a randomised controlled trial', *Prevention Science*, 22:8, pp. 1,120–1,133

Taylor J, Stalker K, Fry D and Steward A (2014) *Disabled Children and Child Protection in Scotland: An investigation into the relationship between professional practice, child protection and disability*, Edinburgh: Scottish Government

Taylor D and Daniel B (eds) (2006) *Child Neglect: Practice issues for health and social care*, London: Jessica Kingsley Publishers

The Fostering Network (undated) *Head, Heart, Hands: Introducing social pedagogy into foster care*, available at: https://bit.ly/3Xrld71

The Fostering Network (2021) *State of the Nation's Foster Care 2021*, available at: https://www.thefosteringnetwork.org.uk/sotn21

The Fostering Network (2022) *Allegations in Foster Care*, available at: https://bit.ly/3w1nSsA

The Prince's Trust (2017) *From Care to Independence: Findings from research supported by The Big Lottery, conducted in partnership with The Prince's Trust*, available at: https://bit.ly/3mYkUUf

Truman P (2004) 'Problems in identifying cases of child neglect', *Nursing Standard*, 18:29, pp. 33–38

Tucker S (2011) 'Listening and believing: an examination of young people's perceptions of why they are not believed by professionals when they report abuse and neglect', *Children & Society*, 25:6, pp. 458–469

Turney D (2000) 'The feminising of neglect', *Child & Family Social Work*, 5, pp. 47–56

Turney D (2016) 'Child neglect and black children' in Bernard C and Harris P (eds) *Safeguarding Black Children: Good practice in child protection*, London: Jessica Kingsley Publishers, pp. 128–145

Twardosz S and Lutzker JR (2010) 'Child maltreatment and the developing brain: a review of neuroscience perspectives', *Aggression and Violent Behaviour*, 15, pp. 59–68

UK Fostering (2022) *When Foster Children Move on*, available at: https://ukfostering.org.uk/when-foster-children-move-on/

Vaughan J and Burnell A (2021) *Parenting a Child with Food and Eating Issues*, London: CoramBAAF

Wales Safeguarding Procedures (2021) *All Wales Child Protection Procedures Practice Guide: Safeguarding children from neglect*, available at: https://www.safeguarding.wales/chi/c6/c6.p5.html

Welsh Government (2016a) *Child Poverty Strategy: Assessment of progress 2016, summary report*, Merthyr Tydfil: Welsh Government

Welsh Government (2016b) *Local Authority Child Protection Registers Wales 2016. Statistics for Wales bulletin 25 November 2016*, Cardiff: Stats Wales

Welsh Government (2021a) *An Integrated Approach to Improving Educational Outcomes for Looked After Children in Wales*, available at: https://bit.ly/3ZwMJSE

Welsh Government (2021b) *Framework on Embedding a Whole School Approach to Emotional and Mental Well-Being*, available at: https://bit.ly/3XtZImh

What Works for Children's Social Care (2022) *New Funding Announced to Run and Evaluate Programmes in Schools to Improve Safeguarding and Educational Outcomes for Children with a Social Worker*, available at: https://bit.ly/3ZstoBT

Wilkinson J and Bower S (2017) *The Impacts of Abuse and Neglect on Children; and Comparisons of Different Placement Options: Evidence review*, London: DfE and RIP

GOOD PRACTICE GUIDES

CoramBAAF's Good Practice Guides are written by experienced practitioners and academics. They explore the legislative and policy framework, research findings and practice experience regarding each topic and use case studies to highlight practice dilemmas and good practice points.

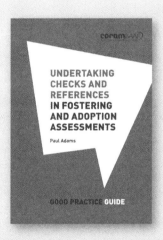

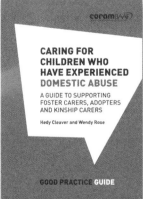

To find out more visit www.corambaaf.org.uk/bookshop